NEW ZEALAND

Roselynn Smelt

MARSHALL CAVENDISH
New York • London • Sydney

Reference edition published 1998 by
Marshall Cavendish Corporation
99 White Plains Road
Tarrytown
New York 10591

© Times Editions Pte Ltd 1998

Originated and designed by
Times Books International, an imprint of
Times Editions Pte Ltd

Printed in Singapore

Library of Congress Cataloging-in-Publication Data:
Smelt, Roselynn.
    New Zealand / Roselynn Smelt.
      p. cm.—(Cultures of the World)
    Includes bibliographical references and index.
    Summary: Introduces the geography, history, religion,
government, economy, and culture of a Pacific island country
first populated by the Maori, to whom it was the "Land of the
Long White Cloud."
    ISBN 0-7614-0808-8 (lib. bdg.)
    1. New Zealand—Juvenile literature. [1. New Zealand.]
I. Title. II. Series.
DU408.S56 1998
993—dc21   97–42179
                  CIP
                  AC

INTRODUCTION

THE LAND OF NEW ZEALAND has shaped its people, as the people have struggled to shape the land. Its two main cultures, as distinct as the forested mountains from the crystal clear lakes and roaring rivers, are united by the rugged land they have conquered and tamed and yet have been divided by it.

Maori ("MAA-or-i") and Pakeha (white New Zealanders) are working together to settle remaining land claims arising out of the legacy left to them by the British colonizers and the Treaty of Waitangi in 1840. As old wounds are healed, New Zealand is becoming a nation more at peace with itself. Long since free of its colonial ties to Britain, New Zealand has emerged as a confident and significant player on the world stage. This book in the *Cultures of the World* series takes a look at the important aspects of New Zealand life that help to define its identity as a dynamic, independent young nation.

CONTENTS

A Maori carving in the meeting house in Waitangi.

CONTENTS

A happy hedge in the town of Tauranga on the North Island.

GEOGRAPHY

NEW ZEALAND, consisting of the North and South Islands, Stewart Island, and several smaller islands, lies about 1,000 miles (1,600 km) southeast of Australia and 1,400 miles (2,300 km) north of Antarctica.

With a total land area of 104,453 square miles (270,534 sq. km), the country is about the size of Colorado. Stretching over 1,000 miles (1,600 km) from north to south and some 280 miles (450 km) across, these slim islands exhibit an amazing diversity of scenery and an impressively long coastline.

Between the subtropical waters of the north and the sub-Antarctic ocean of the south there are about 7,450 miles (12,000 km) of coastline. Spectacular harbors are found in this often indented and unspoiled coastline, which is more than half the coastal length of the United States. The two main islands, North and South, are separated by Cook Strait, which at its narrowest point is about 12 miles (20 km) wide.

Because they are close to the international dateline, Chatham Island (lying off the east coast of the South Island) and the town of Gisborne on the eastern side of the North Island are among the first settlements in the world to see the dawn of a new day.

Left: **Rocky beach along Hauraki Gulf, North Island. For every million New Zealanders, there are over 1,800 miles (3,000 km) of coast, compared with less than 62 miles (100 km) for every million Americans.**

Opposite: **New Zealand has vast areas of undeveloped mountainous land and rivers.**

7

Mount Cook, in the Southern Alps, is the tallest mountain in the country. Standing at a majestic 12,313 feet (3,753 m), it has inspired Maori people to call it Aorangi ("ah-or-rung-ee"), the "cloud piercer." There are more than 200 named peaks higher than 7,500 feet (2,300 m) in New Zealand.

MOUNTAINS, GLACIERS, AND FJORDS

On the geological time scale New Zealand is a relatively young country with most of the modern landscape developing in the last 10 million years. Huge land upheavals deep in the earth 20 million years ago and even earlier caused mountains to be gradually pushed up. At least 75% of the land is 650 feet (200 m) above sea level. The height of the Southern Alps, a massive mountain chain running almost the entire length of the South Island, continues to grow today at the same rate as fingernails.

Mount Taranaki (also known as Mount Egmont) is an extinct volcano with a symmetrical cone, standing in splendid isolation on the west coast of the lower North Island. According to Maori mythology, Taranaki once belonged with the other mountains in the center of the North Island. He wooed and won the wife of Tongariro, another mountain. After a great battle involving fire, steam, and hurling of rocks, Taranaki was banished to the west coast. The path of his escape is said to be marked by the Wanganui River.

The mountains were eroded by glaciers during the Ice Age, which began about 2.5 million years ago. These glaciers (there are 360 in the Southern Alps) carved out the fjords and valleys around most of the South Island lakes and rivers and deposited sediment to form rich alluvial plains, which run down to the sea. The largest, Tasman Glacier, is 18 miles (29 km) long. The fjords are found in the southwestern region of the South Island in an area covered by the Fjordland National Park, one of the largest national parks in the world.

Rugged mountain walls rise almost vertically from the deep calm fjords with breathtaking grandeur. At their highest, these mountain peaks, their walls cascading with waterfalls, can reach over 8,200 feet (2,500 m).

Mount Ruapehu in the Tongariro National Park erupted many times during the winters of 1995 and 1996, causing ash to fall on nearby towns and villages and also seriously disrupting the ski season. This was the first time since 1945 that Ruapehu had erupted.

VOLCANOES AND EARTHQUAKES

New Zealand is positioned on the southwest corner of the so-called "Ring of Fire." This is the area around the rim of the Pacific Ocean where huge sections of the earth's crust called plates collide, causing intense volcanic and earthquake activity.

Compared to other countries on the Pacific rim, such as Japan, the Philippines, and Chile, New Zealand experiences only moderate volcanic and earthquake activity, although minor earthquakes are common. The most disastrous earthquake in recent times occurred in the North Island town of Napier in 1931 when the entire town and surrounding villages were destroyed and 255 people died.

There are many volcanoes in New Zealand, but most are extinct. A volcanic plateau covers most of the central North Island where the mountains of the Tongariro National Park rise. These mountains include three active volcanoes.

LAKES AND RIVERS

There are at least 20 large lakes in New Zealand and many smaller ones. Lake Taupo in the central North Island is by far the biggest at 230 square miles (600 square km). It was formed by an enormous volcanic explosion in A.D. 186 when an incredible 3,600 cubic miles (15,000 cubic km) of ash and pumice fell over virtually all the North Island.

The magnificent alpine settings of the large lakes in the southwestern region of the South Island attract many visitors. Some artificial lakes have been created in both islands to service hydroelectric projects. Numerous rivers speed their way down from the mountains to the sea. Because they are so fast-flowing they have become an important source of hydroelectric power. The longest is the Waikato in the North Island, which flows 264 miles (425 km) into the Tasman Sea.

LOWLANDS

The most extensive flat area in New Zealand, the Canterbury Plains, lies along the eastern coast of the South Island. This is one of the richest farming areas, as the soil is the result of millions of years of glacial deposits. Farms here are the country's main providers of wheat and grain, while the many sheep farms have made the area famous for "Canterbury Lamb." There are also coastal plains in Southland and the Otago provinces. A number of coastal plains are in the North Island: Bay of Plenty province produces dairy cattle and a wide range of subtropical crops, while East Cape produces the bulk of the country's corn. East Cape, Hawke's Bay, and Marlborough in the South Island all have vineyards and orchards.

Lake Taupo—tranquil to-day, but nearly 2,000 years ago, its violent birth saw the spewing of some 15,000 times the volume of material ejected by Mount Saint Helens in Washington state during its eruption in 1980.

Thermal pools in Rotorua. They are a popular attraction for visitors from all over the world.

THERMAL REGION

From south of Lake Taupo to White Island (an active volcano in the Bay of Plenty) is a belt of geysers, boiling mud pools, and hot-water springs, one of which is the world's largest, called Frying Pan Lake. The spring has a surface area of 45,450 square yards (38,000 square meters) and at its deepest point the temperature reaches 389°F (200°C). Much of the thermal activity takes place in and around the city of Rotorua.

Only two other countries have geysers—Iceland and the United States. Geysers occur in areas where water from lakes and rivers seeps down into concentrations of hot rock, heats up rapidly in a confined space, and then explodes up vents as boiling water and steam. The water expelled by the geysers contains dissolved minerals; these solidify into colorful and shapely silica formations on nearby surfaces as water evaporates. It is claimed that the minerals in thermal waters are beneficial and Rotorua has been a therapeutic bathing center of international repute since the late 19th century.

CLIMATE

New Zealand's ocean environment keeps the climate mild, but the mountains, together with the prevailing westerly winds, cause marked differences in temperature and rainfall from west to east. This is particularly so in the South Island where the westerly winds cause the clouds to draw moisture from the sea. As they rise, the clouds hit the mountains and rain is released onto the west coast. Fjordland is one of the wettest areas in the world.

Drought often occurs on the east coast of both islands during the summer months (December–February). However there is usually plenty of rain throughout the whole country with winter (June–August) being the wettest season in the North Island and spring (September–November) being the wettest season on the South Island's west coast. The provinces of Auckland and Northland enjoy a year-round subtropical climate where citrus fruit is grown.

Mean annual temperatures range from 59°F (15°C) in Northland to 50°F (10°C) in the southernmost part of the country. The highest temperatures occur east of the ranges during summer, creating hot and dry conditions, while the lowest temperatures occur during winter in the mountains and the inland areas of Canterbury and Otago. There are few places where temperatures higher than 94.5°F (35°C) or lower than 14°F (−10°C) occur. Snow falls mainly in the mountains, although during the coldest month of the year (July), snow often falls for a few days in eastern coastal provinces of the South Island.

Thriving vegetation and pristine streams—the result of abundant rainfall. New Zealand is a sunny country with most places receiving at least 2,000 hours of sunshine annually.

Mount Cook National Park. Areas of New Zealand with very beautiful, unique, or scientifically important natural features, or containing rare or endangered animals and plants, are preserved and protected as national parks.

FLORA AND FAUNA

Before New Zealand was inhabited by people, the land was covered in forest and "bush" (evergreen, broadleaf trees, and enormous tree ferns, ground ferns, and clinging vines). In the forests, native trees such as rimu ("ri-moo"), totara ("TOR-tah-rah"), and kauri ("kah-oo-ree") grew to spectacular heights.

When the Maori people came to New Zealand around 1,100 years ago, they cleared one third of the forests and later (in the mid-19th century) the European settlers cleared another third. Today, 23% of New Zealand's original forest cover remains. Other tree species have been introduced and the plantation forests now include radiata pine, elm, birch, poplar, macrocarpa, and beech.

Other native vegetation includes coastal wetlands where marine birds such as oyster-catchers and migratory waders can be found and where, in Northland, mangrove trees grow in swamps, mudflats, estuaries, and tidal creeks. New Zealand shrubland contains the highest proportion of tree-sized daisies and plants with inter-locking and twisted branches in the world. In the grasslands can be found toi-toi, pampas, and flax plants, which were cultivated by the early Maori and used to make baskets and clothing, thatching for their houses, and ropes, sails, and rigging for their ships.

Because New Zealand was cut off by its oceans from the rest of the world over 80 million years ago, only mammals that could fly were able to reach it. The only native land mammal is the bat; other land mammals were introduced by the Maori and European settlers.

THE KIWI

The kiwi ("ki-wee"), a large, nocturnal, and shy flightless bird, has a long slender bill with nostrils at the tip. It lays only one egg, which is the largest egg in relation to body size of all birds, at approximately one-third the female bird's weight. After the egg is laid the male partner incubates and rears the young. It is the only bird with a sense of smell. Its name comes from the male bird's distinctive, shrill call. The kiwi is a well-known emblem of New Zealand, appearing on its one dollar coin. It is also a popular nickname for a New Zealander.

Nearly all New Zealand's native species of reptiles and amphibians live nowhere else in the world. New Zealand's native frogs lay eggs that turn directly into frogs without first becoming free-swimming tadpoles. They have tail-wagging muscles, but no tails, and they don't have a call. These unusual features place them among the world's most ancient frogs.

Of 44 reptile species that are native to New Zealand, the tuatara ("too-uh-tah-ruh") is the largest, growing up to two feet (60 cm). It is the only surviving species of a family of reptiles that became extinct in other parts of the world 100 million years ago. Found only on New

Zealand's offshore islands, the tuatara (which resembles an iguana) has traces of what was once a third eye. Tuatara are aggressive predators, ambushing their prey with spectacular bursts of speed and strength. It is one of the rarest reptiles on earth.

An even more ancient "living fossil" is New Zealand's weta ("we-tah"), a wingless insect that has hardly changed at all in the last 190 million years. The harmless giant weta is the heaviest insect in the world, weighing up to 2 1/2 ounces (71 grams), almost as much as a thrush.

New Zealand also has one of the world's largest gecko lizards. It is unlike any other species in the world (except one in New Caledonia) in that it does not lay eggs but gives live birth to its young—usually twins.

Before mammals were introduced, flightless birds (including very large species) were able to exist without threat. Moa ("maw-ah") became extinct in pre-European times, but large flightless birds still remain, including the kiwi, the kakapo ("KUH-KUH-POR"), the heaviest parrot in the world, and the weka ("we-ka"), an inquisitive bush-hen. The kea ("ke-uh") (see photo) is the only alpine parrot in the world.

Scene in the South Island province of Canterbury. New Zealand's population of 3.6 million (about the same as Houston or Boston) is very small compared to other countries of similar land size. Japan, for example, has a population of 124.8 million. Some 85% of New Zealanders live in centers with 1,000 or more people. Only 15% live in rural areas.

PROVINCES AND CITIES

When the European settlers came to New Zealand in the mid-19th century, they mostly settled in the South Island. But for the last 100 years, people have been drifting north, and now 2.7 million people (75% of the population) live in the North Island, with 48% concentrated in the provinces of Northland, Auckland, Waikato, and Bay of Plenty, where the climate is warmer.

There are four main urban centers: Auckland and Wellington in the North Island and Christchurch and Dunedin in the South Island.

AUCKLAND New Zealand's largest urban area occupies the isthmus between the Hauraki Gulf on the east coast and the Manukau Harbor on the west coast. With about one boat for every four households, Auckland has earned the name "City of Sails." A city of over one million inhabitants, it is the most cosmopolitan place in the country and is the main tourist and trade gateway.

WELLINGTON CABLE CAR

WELLINGTON, the capital of New Zealand, is located near the southern end of the North Island. It is the second largest urban area, with a population of 326,000. Wellington Harbor in Port Nicholson covers 7 square miles (18 sq. km) and is considered one of the finest deep-water harbors in the world.

CHRISTCHURCH is situated on the Canterbury Plains. It has a population of 310,000. Early English settlers were successful in recreating an English society in Christchurch. This is reflected in the city's English layout with a stone, Gothic-style Anglican cathedral dominating a central square.

DUNEDIN has a population of 110,000 and is sited at the top of the long, fjord-like Otago Harbor. Settled originally by people from Scotland, Dunedin was named after the old Celtic name of Edinburgh, Dun Edin, and is sometimes called the "Edinburgh of the South." It is here that New Zealand's only whisky is distilled.

Wellington is the country's administrative, financial, and cultural center. A cable car links the downtown area to the hilltop Victoria University from where the views are magnificent.

HISTORY

AS THE LAST SIGNIFICANT LAND MASS in the world to be populated, New Zealand's history is relatively short. Until the late 19th century the inhabitants of New Zealand, known as the Maori, transferred their history down the generations largely by word-of-mouth. Some events may have become distorted over time, but other things are known for certain.

Europeans first sighted New Zealand in the 17th century and by the early 19th century British settlers had arrived. New Zealand became a British colony in 1840 with the signing of the Waitangi Treaty and by 1907 it was constituted as a Dominion in the British empire.

Although New Zealand has now become less dependent on Britain, it remains a member of the British Commonwealth.

Above: **A replica of an early Maori canoe. When white settlers arrived in New Zealand, Maoridom was divided into 42 distinct tribal groups. They had no concept of nationhood and no name for themselves, only tribal names. To distinguish themselves from the Europeans (who were different), they called themselves Maori, meaning ordinary or usual. The Maori called Europeans Pakeha ("PAA-ke-haa")—"white stranger."**

Opposite: **The statue of an honored New Zealand soldier, F.W. Wylie, in Government Gardens, Rotorua.**

EARLY ARRIVALS

The first people to come to New Zealand, in about the 10th century A.D., were from eastern Polynesia—known to them as Hawaiki. Some historians believe there was a "Great Migration" at one point in time, while other evidence suggests that numerous canoe voyages from Hawaiki brought groups of Polynesians to New Zealand over a period of hundreds of years. The occupants of these famous canoes became the founders of Maori tribes that still exist today.

According to a Maori legend, the very first voyager to reach New Zealand, in about A.D. 950, was a man called Kupe. He named the country Aotearoa ("ah-or-te-ah-roar"), which means "land of the long white cloud." Before Kupe arrived, there was no human habitation on the islands.

The nature of each village or settlement varied, depending on the activities taking place within and around it. Horticultural communities lived near their gardens; other groups moved their settlements into the bush to hunt or, if necessary, farther along a coast to fish. Food was stored in communal storehouses in each settlement.

PRE-EUROPEAN MAORI

The Maori brought with them dogs, rats, and edible plants. They subsisted on fishing, hunting (especially the giant moa bird), and gathering plants. Maori people were also pastoralists, growing their own crops such as *kumara* ("KOO-mah-rah"), a sweet potato. They grouped themselves into extended families, subtribes with up to 500 members, and tribes. Each tribe lived in a village usually within reach of an earthwork fort, or *pa* ("PAA").

Tribal land, valued for the food it could produce, such as mutton birds, or its natural resources, such as greenstone, was presided over by tribal chiefs and jealously guarded. While tribes did trade their various regional commodities, intertribal warfare was a way of gaining control over the best land. It also gave *mana* ("mah-nah"), or prestige and honor, to the chiefs.

Early Maori life. Tribal warfare was not uncommon, and after fierce conflict the Maori would eat their defeated enemies. Young women and children were often taken as slaves.

EUROPEAN DISCOVERY

The Dutch navigator Abel Tasman was the first European to sight New Zealand in December 1642. He called it "Staten Landt," but it was soon renamed "Nieuw Zealand" after a Dutch province. Unfortunately, when Tasman attempted to land, the local Maori thought his trumpet fanfare was a call to war and Tasman lost four men. He sailed away without ever landing and never came back.

Europeans did not return to New Zealand until 1769 when Captain James Cook, an English explorer, was sent to the South Pacific on a scientific expedition. He circumnavigated the country and thoroughly surveyed its coastline. His good reports encouraged whalers and traders to come to New Zealand. Other explorers began to arrive, including the French, Italians, and Americans.

By the late 18th century there were probably about 150,000 Maori living in Aotearoa, nearly all of them in the warmer North Island. While they were naturally suspicious of the early Europeans, the Maori were quick to see the advantages in trading with the Europeans, particularly to gain muskets for tribal warfare.

A hand-engraving of Captain James Cook. He was killed by natives in Hawaii in 1779 on his third expedition to the Pacific Ocean.

NEW ARRIVALS

Three Christian missionary families formed the first organized European settlement in the country. The Reverend Samuel Marsden arrived from England in 1814 and preached his first sermon in the Bay of Islands on Christmas Day. By 1838 the Frenchman, Bishop Pompallier, had founded a Roman Catholic Mission in the same area.

The original Bay of Islands church. Missionaries introduced European technology and agricultural skills and thus expected to gain favor and prestige with the Maori people. They also hoped to influence trade between the whalers and the Maori. But the sophisticated Maori chiefs got the best deals and directly controlled trade.

The vision of the early missionaries was for a Christian and Maori New Zealand. However, commercial interests were to dominate subsequent developments. In 1839 Edward Gibbon Wakefield formed the New Zealand Company. It was directed by influential men in London commerce, who were eager to get the economy going. They dispatched settlers to Aotearoa and profited by selling their newly acquired land to them.

By the 1840s there were about 2,000 Europeans living in small settlements in New Zealand. Scattered throughout the country was a large transient population of whalers and traders. The Maori population, divided into independent tribes, had hardly changed since the late 1700s. They traded extensively and successfully with the Europeans.

There was, however, no national government, no one set of formal laws, and Maori land was being sold in a disorganized way. Some British settlers feared that New Zealand might be taken over by France and so both Maori and Pakeha (white New Zealander) groups asked Britain to provide some sort of protection and law and order.

INDEPENDENCE AND A TREATY

Britain accepted the Maori chiefs' request to recognize their independence, while at the same time extending Crown protection to New Zealand. It was hoped that British Resident James Busby would bring about law and order in the country. Unfortunately he lacked the means to enforce his authority and, as more and more emigrants arrived in New Zealand, disagreements between Maori and Pakeha began to threaten lives and trade. Busby was replaced by William Hobson, a naval captain, who was sent to New Zealand in January 1840 to negotiate with the Maori for the sovereignty of the country.

Britain decided to make a colony of New Zealand in order to control the European settlers and protect the rights of the Maori people. Hobson, Busby, and the missionary Henry Williams conceived the idea of drawing up a treaty that would be acceptable to the Crown and the Maori chiefs. On February 6, 1840, at Waitangi in the Bay of Islands, a treaty was read out in English and Maori to over 400 Maori. After much debate and on the advice of Williams, the Maori chiefs agreed to the Queen of England having sovereignty over their land. They accepted her protection and the offer of the same rights and duties of citizenship as the people of England, while still retaining possession of their lands, forests, fisheries, and other possessions. Over 40 signatures or marks were appended to the Maori text of the treaty, mostly by chiefs around the Bay of Islands. The Maori version of the Treaty of Waitangi was eventually signed by more than 500 chiefs.

For the Maori people the Treaty of Waitangi recognized that in exchange for settlement rights, their natural rights as original occupants would be upheld. For the European settlers the treaty allowed them to emigrate peacefully to New Zealand under the British flag.

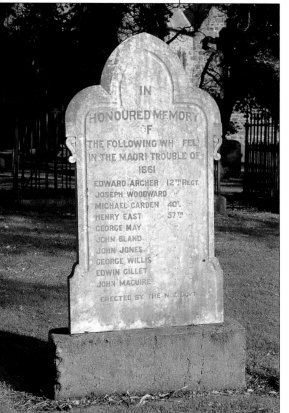

A tombstone commemorates soldiers who died in the Maori land wars of the 1860s.

LAND WARS

At first the treaty was recognized and observed as a contract binding on both parties, and in 1852 Britain allowed New Zealand to be self-governing. As people continued to migrate to New Zealand, there was increasing demand for land, and Maori people became cautious about selling their land cheaply to investors who profited from the settlers.

The law seemed to favor the Pakeha. Conflict between settlers and Maori finally led to the land wars of the 1860s and the emergence of united tribes in the central North Island with their own king. (The area is still known today as "King Country.") Thousands of British troops were dispatched to control the Maori. It was at this stage that New Zealand became a British colony in reality, not just on paper.

GROWING PROSPERITY

Peace was not restored until 1870. Meanwhile, the discovery of gold in 1861 at Gabriels Gully, Otago saw the beginning of a major gold rush in New Zealand. A flood of new settlers came to the South Island, which was relatively untroubled by land disputes. The gold rush was all over by the 1870s, but by then agricultural industries had developed that could employ the growing population. Railways and roads were built so that produce could be transported to the coast and shipped all over the world. The discovery of refrigeration in the 1880s meant that meat and dairy products could travel as far as England.

DEVELOPING SENSE OF NATIONHOOD

New Zealand became a Dominion in 1907. At the outbreak of World War I in 1914, the country remained loyal to Great Britain by sending troops to Europe. New Zealand lost 17,000 men from a population of only one million, due largely to a badly organized campaign by the British in Turkey. New Zealanders began to be disenchanted with the "motherland" and a sense of separate nationhood began to grow.

A period of industrial progress followed in the 1920s, but the worldwide Depression of the 1930s hit New Zealand severely. The Labor Party, which had been formed out of various labor, trade union, and radical movements, won an election and formed its first government in 1935 under Michael Joseph Savage.

There followed a number of social reforms, including a social security system, a national health service, and a low-rent state housing program. The National Party also emerged during this period to represent more conservative and rural interests. It won its first election in 1949. Since

New Zealand and Australian troops bound for Europe during World War I.

A Dominion is a self-governing country of the British empire; a colony is ruled directly by the British government.

25

Robert Muldoon concentrated economic and political power in his own hands. With his ruthless and abrasive style and quick wit, he dominated Parliament and his own cabinet ministers.

1949 Labor and National parties have competed in elections to form the government, the Labor Party holding power for 13 years and the National Party for 35 years, sometimes in coalition with minor parties.

The early, post-World War II years saw a boom in New Zealand because of higher prices for wool as well as other agricultural products. The Korean War was on, and there was a demand for blankets in that country. The boom ended with the end of the Korean War.

Changes in the world economy during the 1960s and 1970s threatened New Zealand's high standard of living. When Great Britain joined the European Economic Community in 1973, New Zealand lost guaranteed access on favorable terms to its largest overseas market. The same year, a worldwide oil crisis threatened oil supplies to New Zealand and, from 1974, the impact of much higher world oil prices was felt. New Zealand's traditional economic and political relations were challenged.

In 1975 a leader emerged who was determined to tackle the crisis. Robert Muldoon, the new National Party prime minister, extended protection to the manufacturing industry and increased government funding to the troubled farming sector. To help the economy grow, his government funded an array of expensive "Think Big" projects. To counter inflation, Muldoon assumed increasing controls. By 1984 the government was setting all prices and wages, as well as interest rates and the exchange rate between the New Zealand dollar and other currencies. New Zealand had become one of the most centrally controlled economies in the world.

CRISIS

Huge and growing economic and political pressures resulted. In 1984 Muldoon called a general election, which his National Party lost to the Labor Party. The new government faced a massive economic crisis.

The New Zealand dollar was devalued and over the next six years, the Labor government began a major program of deregulation and financial reform. By the early 1990s, New Zealand was assessed by the World Bank and other international organizations as having one of the most deregulated and least centrally controlled economies in the world.

NUCLEAR FREE

By reducing the role of government, the Labor government of 1984–90 departed from many traditional Labor Party policies. But on one subject, they held to election promises: a nuclear-free New Zealand. The government refused to accept visits from American or other warships that might be carrying nuclear weapons or that were nuclear-powered.

The Labor Prime Minister David Lange made the nuclear-free position his personal crusade. Eventually, increasing tensions within the Labor government over the reforms and their impact on the poor marred the later years of his leadership. Lange resigned from the premiership in 1990 and Labor lost the 1990 and 1993 elections to the National Party.

A reformed National Party, free of the influence of Robert Muldoon, continued the reform process and built on the growing acceptance at home and abroad of both New Zealand's radical economic reforms and its nuclear-free position.

Despite pressure from the United States and French governments, David Lange kept New Zealand nuclear-free. An outstanding orator, he once won an internationally televised debate at the Oxford Union in England on the subject.

GOVERNMENT

NEW ZEALAND IS AN INDEPENDENT STATE with a democratic form of government. It is a member of the British Commonwealth, Asia-Pacific Economic Cooperation (APEC), and the United Nations and associated bodies.

HEAD OF STATE

The formal head of state is Queen Elizabeth II of Great Britain. The queen is represented in New Zealand by the governor-general, who is appointed by the queen on the advice of the New Zealand government, normally for three to five years. Early governor-generals were often nobility from England. More recently, they have been distinguished New Zealanders.

As the queen's representative, the governor-general opens Parliament, formally appoints the prime minister and ministers, and signs legislation passed by Parliament. The governor-general has no discretion in such matters, accepting the advice of the prime minister and government of the day. Only where there is no clear control of Parliament, and thus no clear government, would the governor-general have more than a nominal role to play.

In recent years, there has been some discussion of whether New Zealand should become a republic, replacing the sovereign with a government-appointed head of state. Effectively, this would raise the governor-general to the status of president, rather than a representative of the queen. Opinion polls indicate that most New Zealanders prefer to retain the queen as head of state.

Above: **An enthusiastic crowd greets Queen Elizabeth II during an official visit to New Zealand.**

Opposite: **The Parliament building in Wellington.**

29

The Rotorua municipal building.

AN UNUSUALLY SIMPLE STRUCTURE

Due to a number of features, New Zealand has possibly one of the simplest structures of government of any advanced nation:

NO WRITTEN CONSTITUTION Like Great Britain, New Zealand is a parliamentary sovereignty—that is, the will of Parliament rules supreme. The laws that Parliament makes are the rule of law for the country and the role of the courts is only to interpret them.

NO SEPARATION OF POWERS The party or coalition of parties that controls Parliament decides who will be appointed as prime minister and as ministers. Each minister is given an area or areas of responsibility. The departments of government (the executive) covering that area report to and are responsible to the minister concerned. In other words, the group that controls Parliament also controls the executive. The judiciary is independent, but it cannot overturn laws passed by Parliament. Thus, it too is subject to laws passed by the group that controls Parliament.

ONLY ONE CHAMBER OF PARLIAMENT In 1950 the second chamber of Parliament was abolished. The single chamber consists of elected members of Parliament, and control of it—by winning—gives control of Parliament.

LOCAL GOVERNMENT RELATIVELY UNIM-PORTANT Local and regional government account for less than 2% of economic activity in New Zealand. Unlike in many countries, local authorities have no direct role in the provision of education or health services—these are the responsibility of the central government.

Elected local and regional government bodies are responsible for sewerage, water supply, flood control, local roads (but not national highways), planning controls (for example, changes of land use and building permits), and provision of optional local leisure facilities such as a sports stadium.

Until recently, local authorities controlled ports and electricity distribution. This is no longer required by law and many local authorities have sold or part-sold their interest to private owners. The main source of revenue for local and regional government is property tax.

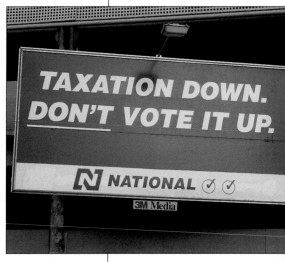

Taxes are always a contentious issue in elections.

FIRST-PAST-THE-POST ELECTORAL SYSTEM Until the October 1996 general election, members were elected to Parliament by direct election from constituencies around the country. This usually meant that one party would win control of Parliament.

In this winner-take-all system, called a first-past-the-post system in New Zealand, votes cast for losing candidates were not reflected in the make-up of Parliament. Unhappiness with this system eventually resulted in a call for change from a first-past-the-post electoral system to one of proportional representation.

Due to the efforts of Kate Sheppard, New Zealand, on September 19, 1893, became the first country in the world to allow women to vote.

A NEW ELECTORAL SYSTEM

In two referenda in 1992 and 1993, New Zealanders voted to adopt a system of proportional representation for Parliament called "mixed member proportional" (MMP).

Under the old system, minor parties could gain a significant minority of votes, but not win any individual seats in Parliament. Under MMP, the number of seats a party gains in Parliament is dictated by the proportion of the vote it receives nationally.

ELECTION RESULTS: FIRST MMP GOVERNMENT

The first MMP election held in October 1996 left a third party, New Zealand First, holding the balance of power between Labor and National. After lengthy negotiations, New Zealand First entered a formal coalition with the National Party in December 1996. Jim Bolger, the leader of the National Party, remained prime minister.

JIM BOLGER

Prime Minister Jim Bolger repeatedly emphasizes his pragmatic approach to politics. In the 1990 election, Labor had suffered two changes of leadership and the country found the pragmatic approach of Bolger and the National Party more attractive. National gained an absolute majority.

In 1993 National's share of seats was reduced and Bolger could only govern with the support of minor parties. In 1996, under the new MMP system, National's share of seats was reduced further, but Bolger was able to remain prime minister by entering a formal coalition with the New Zealand First party.

PARLIAMENT

Parliament is responsible for making laws, voting "supply" (finance) to the government, and providing the ministerial heads of the executive.

Proposed laws are placed before Parliament in the form of bills. These are debated both on the floor of the house and, generally, by a subcommittee of members of Parliament (MPs). A successful bill has to pass through three "readings," or votes in Parliament, before being sent to the governor-general for signature and passage into law. Most bills are introduced by the government of the day, although the opposition or individual MPs may seek to introduce bills, too.

Each year, the budget contains the government's proposals for expenditure and for revenue-raising. This is specified in great detail in budget documents prepared by the Treasury for the government. Until recently, the budget was voted on in its entirety by the government-controlled majority of MPs. Individual MPs were not permitted to make proposals for changes to the budget.

However, as part of the move to proportional representation, these rules have been changed so that individual MPs can now make such proposals, provided they do not significantly alter the budget. New Zealand is the first country with an advanced economy to allow its Parliament to do this.

Most matters are settled along party lines, with the party leadership deciding how members of that party should vote. On some issues, however, MPs vote as matters of conscience—for instance, private members' bills to permit casinos (passed) and to permit euthanasia (rejected).

A REFORMED EXECUTIVE

Although reforms have increased accountability, they have also reduced loyalty and the body of experience in the public sector, with junior staff and chief executives alike tending to move between departments and in and out of the public service.

Executive government is carried out under the control of the ministers appointed by the governor-general—in practice, those chosen by the party or parties controlling Parliament.

There are some 34,000 staff employed by public service departments. The public service was substantially reorganized as part of widespread economic reforms in the 1980s. These reforms have greatly increased flexibility and accountability and sharpened efficiency. Under the State Sector Act 1988, the chief executive of each public department is now accountable for running his or her department efficiently and effectively and agrees on a contract of performance with the minister in charge of that department.

In this contractual relationship between ministers and department chief executives, the ministers decide what results they want and how much money is available. As in private sector firms, chief executives determine how they will accomplish the job, and they have a large degree of freedom in this role.

Financial reforms in the Public Finance Act and elsewhere have required public departments to provide a high standard of financial

PRIVATIZATION

Many public sector trading activities, including New Zealand Telecom and Post Bank, have been sold to the private sector. Of the remainder, many have been formed into State Owned Enterprises (SOEs). These are commercial bodies run by directors with extensive business experience. The objective is to make a profit, with the government as a shareholder. The idea is to keep ministers' involvement with SOEs to the minimum. In practice, key SOE decisions (for example, over some electricity charges) are politically sensitive and tend to trigger ministers' involvement.

disclosure, for instance in distinguishing current expenditure from capital (investment) expenditure.

In public sector reforms and accountability, New Zealand is recognized as a world leader. The system has been much studied by overseas delegations and international bodies.

THE JUDICIARY

Judges interpret and apply the law, and the judiciary is independent of the government.

Aside from a system of district courts and the High Court, there are various specialist tribunals and courts. Most notable are the Employment Court and Tribunal (to consider employment disputes) and the Waitangi Tribunal (to consider claims arising under the Treaty of Waitangi).

A police officer makes his rounds.

The most senior court in New Zealand is the Court of Appeal. Appeals from lower courts can be made to this body, while appeals from the Court of Appeal can be made to the Privy Council in England. However, the Privy Council, in reaching its verdicts, is bound by New Zealand statute.

The main form of law in New Zealand is New Zealand statute law, that is, law passed by the New Zealand Parliament. Subject to this are three other forms of law: common law (case law based on general rules developed by the courts, not only in New Zealand, but also, where relevant, in England and in other Commonwealth countries); United Kingdom statutes; and subordinate legislation (New Zealand statute may delegate some law-making powers to the governor-general and to local government).

ECONOMY

NEW ZEALAND HAS AN ADVANCED ECONOMY. From the 1860s onward, it offered a high standard of living to most European settlers, so that an ordinary working-class family could enjoy daily meat on the table and a horse for transportation when these would have been but dreams for such people in Europe. New Zealand's position relative to other advanced economies has slowly declined during the 20th century. Nonetheless, the World Bank calculates that, allowing for differences in prices between New Zealand and other countries, the income per person in New Zealand in 1994 was equivalent to US$16,000, slightly lower than that of Great Britain and two-thirds that of the United States.

The primary economic sector—agriculture, forestry, and fishing—accounts for around 10% of New Zealand's production and employment, and manufacturing for about 20%. Thus, the lion's share of production and employment is in the service sector.

Electricity prices in New Zealand are among the lowest in the world. This is because two thirds of the supply comes from hydroelectric power. Cheap power is particularly important to the aluminum smelting industry, since its major cost is electricity.

Left and opposite: **Only a minority of jobs in New Zealand now demand physical strength. Rapid economic change has removed the expectation of a job for life and most New Zealanders work hard and play hard.**

37

The largest employers in New Zealand are community, social, and personal services (423,000 employees) and trade, restaurants, and hotels (329,000 employees).

THE REFORMS

The success of New Zealand's major economic reforms from the mid-1980s to early 1990s is subject to much debate, both domestically and internationally—New Zealand being a test case for radical reform. The reforms caused big structural changes in New Zealand, particularly since they followed a period of tight state control.

The reforms began with the removal of exchange and loan controls, the deregulation of financial markets, and the floating of the New Zealand dollar. Subsidies to farming were virtually eliminated, making New Zealand agriculture the least subsidized in the world. Import controls were removed and tariffs gradually reduced. Free trade with Australia was established in 1989. The domestic air market was opened up, and ports, coastal shipping, and road transportation deregulated.

The public sector was reformed and the government's accounts greatly improved, so that they resembled those of a large company. Government-owned trading activities were set up on commercial lines and in many cases, sold. The government received some US$9 billion from privatization between 1988 and 1995.

The Reserve Bank Act of 1989 made the central bank independent of government, with the sole aim of monetary policy being price stability.

The last of the major reforms, the Employment Contracts Act of 1991, decentralized wage negotiations from industry and occupational level to the firm. Trade union membership was made voluntary and workers could now choose which union they wanted to represent them, if any.

The aims of all these reforms were to improve the country's economic performance and the government's financial position. The main initial impact of the reforms was to increase efficiency, but, at the same time, to increase unemployment.

Forestry, mining, railways, postal services, telecommunications, electricity generation and transmission, and other areas had been run as government departments with little concern for profit, return on investment, or for the customer. Under commercial pressures, it proved possible to run these services with far less staff. Typically, employment fell by a third to two-thirds. Organizations such as postal services and railways moved from being loss makers requiring frequent government subsidies to being profitable firms.

A parking meter attendant on duty.

ROGER DOUGLAS—HERO OR TRAITOR?

As the Labor government's finance minister from 1984 to 1988, Roger Douglas was the primary architect of New Zealand's economic reforms, which became known as "Rogernomics."

Because the reforms overturned traditional views about the role of government and led to job losses, he was regarded as a traitor by some Labor Party supporters. Nonetheless, his reforms were welcomed by others as giving the country new hope for the future.

Douglas's proposals became increasingly radical and led to a split with Prime Minister Lange, who fired him. Douglas later left the Labor Party and helped form a new right-wing and reform-minded party called ACT.

A farm woman spins wool. New Zealand is the world's largest producer of "strong wool," which is used mainly for carpets, hand knitting, and blankets.

But tens of thousands of workers lost their jobs. Unemployment climbed from 4% in 1986 to a peak of 11% in 1991. Some rural communities and small towns were devastated, and the large supply of low-skilled but well-paying jobs that had characterized the New Zealand economy for many decades was permanently lost. Many traditional occupations and career paths vanished.

The removal of financial regulations led to a credit and banking boom in the cities. Speculative companies were launched and the stock market rocketed upward. However, the New York stock market crash of October 1987 brought New Zealand's financial bubble to an abrupt end. Many of the banks and financial companies lacked the expertise to make sound investments in the new environment. One big retail bank needed two large capital injections from the government to stay afloat.

Despite these problems, the deregulated economy offered new opportunities. The economy finally moved out of recession in 1993 and most of New Zealand's economic indicators are now good. Its recent past and expected future growth levels are better than most other advanced economies. Inflation and government debt are low and the government has run a budget surplus for several years. Unemployment is below 7%. Private investment has replaced falling government investment.

In these terms, the economic reforms have been a success. However, concerns remain about investment and trade and the social impact of the reforms.

MACROECONOMIC POLICY

After World War II, New Zealand fell into a pattern of high inflation—making New Zealand prices higher relative to those of its trading partners—and repeated currency devaluations that restored New Zealand prices to a lower level, making exports more competitive.

As New Zealand living standards started to fall behind those of other advanced countries, successive governments tried to meet voters' concerns and assist industry by spending more. As government expenditure was consistently higher than its revenue, it had to borrow more and more, and then had to pay interest on its debt. This pushed up government expenditure further, making it even more difficult to balance the books.

The government's net public debt peaked at US$33 billion in 1992, or 51% of Gross Domestic Product (GDP). With subsequent economic growth and restraints and efficiencies in government expenditure, the situation has improved rapidly. By 1996 net public debt had fallen to some US$20 billion, or 32% of GDP.

The central bank has operated a tough anti-inflation policy that has worked, but at the price of high interest rates and exchange rates. In terms of real interest rates (the actual interest rate less inflation), New Zealand has tended to have the highest rates of any advanced economy. This has deterred domestic investment—the cost of borrowing in New Zealand being so high—but attracted funds from overseas. High exchange rates have made exports more expensive overseas and imports into New Zealand cheaper.

Fishermen in Tauranga. A typical catch could include mackerel, tuna, dory, and blue grenadier.

Investment comes from Australia, the United States, and Britain, with a small but growing percentage from Japan and East Asia. It has mainly been targeted at financial services, telecommunications, forestry, and some areas of manufacturing.

FOREIGN INVESTMENT

Since privatization began in 1988, major flows of foreign direct investment (where a company buys a controlling interest in a firm, rather than buys stock or lends money on set terms) have been attracted to New Zealand. As a percentage of GDP, New Zealand has consistently attracted the highest levels of such investment of any advanced economy, often some US$2 billion per year (3–4% of GDP).

The investment brings the capital, managerial skills, and contacts of overseas firms to New Zealand and demonstrates their confidence in the economy. Many overseas managers work in New Zealand. The New Zealand seller (often the government) gains the sale price. But the sale means a loss of control to the foreign investors, who will also look for a return on their investment.

Major investment both directly in forestry and in the processing of forest products is being undertaken by large firms from New Zealand, Japan, the United States, Malaysia, and China. In some rural areas, farmland is being replaced by commercial forests, changing the local communities.

TRADE

As a small economy, less than 1% the size of the United States' economy, New Zealand is highly dependent on trade. With a workforce of 1.6 million, it has to specialize and import many items.

For much of its history, the New Zealand economy has been dominated by the primary sector, that is, agriculture, fishing, forestry, and mining. In 1913 New Zealand's main three exports were (in descending order of importance) wool, meat, and dairy products. In 1983 the same three industries dominated exports, though dairy products had overtaken wool and meat. However, from the 1970s, exports have diversified and now include forestry products, fish, and fruit. The manufacturing sector also grew in importance as an exporter, and tourism became a significant earner of foreign currency.

In 1995 total merchandise exports (which excludes trade in services, such as tourism) were worth US$14 billion, one third from manufactured exports and two thirds from primary sector exports (including food). Key earners of foreign currency were: tourism—US$2.8 billion from overseas visitors (estimated); dairy—US$2.3 billion; meat—US$2 billion; forestry—US$1.7 billion; fish—US$0.8 billion; wool—US$0.7 billion; fruit and nuts—US$550 million; aluminum—US$480 million.

Until the mid-1970s, the main export market for New Zealand was Great Britain. Since then, New Zealand has diversified. Five markets are now of roughly equal importance: Australia, North America, West Europe, Japan, and East Asia.

An abandoned copper mine. The mining and quarrying sector employs about 5,000 workers.

In recent years, New Zealand wines have moved from being low-priced products salable only on the domestic market to international prize winners.

Many of New Zealand's primary and manufacturing exporters have had difficulty in establishing distinctive products overseas. Often, New Zealand exports commodities that have been bought solely on price and with the purchaser indifferent to who supplies them. This means New Zealand is a "price taker," vulnerable to changes in world commodity markets.

However, as the economic reforms have taken effect, some firms and industries have developed distinctive new, high value-added products. For example, a New Zealand manufacturer of dishwashers and washing machines successfully exports to Europe. A manufacturer of aluminum frames has a zero-default work practice, much studied by visiting Japanese delegations. Sophisticated navigational equipment is sold to overseas navies and major airports. Live fish are exported to Japan so that they can be consumed when fresh. Flower exports to East Asia are developing rapidly. New Zealand yacht designers and builders are internationally acclaimed. More such success stories will be needed to ensure that New Zealand's trade continues to grow both in value and sophistication.

A milking demonstration for tourists. New Zealand has over eight million head of cattle.

MAJOR SECTORS

DAIRY New Zealand is one of the major suppliers of dairy products in world markets, which take 90% of the milk produced in New Zealand. The combination of low population density, good infrastructure, and grass that grows rapidly makes New Zealand a highly competitive producer of dairy products. However, the United States and Western European markets strongly protect their local producers, limiting opportunities for New Zealand to penetrate these markets.

The New Zealand Dairy Board markets dairy products overseas and is one of the largest dairy companies in the world. It is seeking to develop markets in Asia and new products for North America and Western Europe. The Dairy Board is owned by the country's regional farm cooperatives. Its monopoly of exports is much debated—while a unified and expert marketing organization offers obvious advantages to the farmers, the negative side is the potential inefficiencies in a monopoly.

Among tourists in New Zealand, the biggest spenders come from Australia, Japan, the United States, and Great Britain.

MEAT AND WOOL Over a quarter of New Zealand's land area is used for sheep farming. There are 14 sheep for every person and most are dual-purpose meat and wool animals. Each year about 30 million lambs and sheep and 3 million cattle are slaughtered in New Zealand. This produces over 500 million tons (455 million metric tons) of lamb and mutton and over 500 million tons of beef and veal. New Zealand's main markets for meat are North America and Western Europe.

TOURISM Tourism grew rapidly during the 1980s and 1990s, with New Zealand's isolation posing less of a barrier to travelers and instead becoming an attraction. Some 1.3 million people visited New Zealand in 1995 and this is expected to grow to two million by the year 2000. Visitor growth has been highest from some East Asian countries, notably South Korea and Taiwan.

Tourism development requires careful handling so as not to overcrowd key sights. New attractions are continually being developed. For example, Queenstown, in the Southern Alps on Lake Wakatipu, has the style of an international ski resort, while offering ready access to wilderness walks, mountain climbing, heli-skiing, bungee-jumping, and white-water rafting (right), among other sports.

FORESTRY Commercial plantation forests (mainly pine) cover about 4% of New Zealand's land area. This is one of the largest concentrations of plantation forest and of softwood in the world. New Zealand expects to supply some 39 million cubic yards (30 million cubic meters) of softwood per year by 2010.

The main commercial tree species, *pinus radiata*, can be harvested on a 27-year cycle—the most rapid of any major supplier. New Zealand accounts for a third of the world's radiata pine.

INFRASTRUCTURE New Zealand's international competitiveness and quality of life for its population partly depends on its infrastructure. With a low density of population, expenditure on roads per person is high. New Zealand relies heavily on sea transportation for overseas trade, although some high value goods, such as flowers and seafood, are air-freighted for freshness to sophisticated markets like Japan.

With deregulation of the ports in 1990, the ports changed from some of the least efficient in the world to some of the most efficient, port costs typically falling by a half to two thirds within two years. With the opening up of domestic air services to competition in 1987, airport and in-flight facilities improved virtually overnight.

New Zealand has the least regulated telecommunications sector in the world. The largest supplier, Telecom, has invested heavily in new technology and prices have fallen rapidly.

The Wairakei thermal power station. New Zealand produces 7% of its electrical power from geothermal fields and hot springs. There are no nuclear power plants. New Zealand is 70% self-sufficient in power.

47

NEW ZEALANDERS

DURING THE FIRST 50 YEARS of European settlement (between 1831 and 1881), the European population of New Zealand increased from fewer than 1,000 people to half a million. In 1886 40% of these Europeans were British, coming from England, Scotland, Wales, and Ireland. They were mostly from laboring and lower-middle-class backgrounds. It was the intention of the New Zealand Company and the government to people New Zealand with Britons—to create a Britain of the South. Over 150 years later New Zealand presents a kaleidoscope of different peoples from Asia, Polynesia, and many other parts of the world.

TOILS AND TITLES

New Zealand was oversold in Great Britain as a "Land of Promise" with very fertile soil, banana plantations, and other tropical fruit orchards. Steep hillsides covered in bush and scrub were described as "perfect for grapevines, wheat, and olives." A few aristocrats also emigrated, hoping to establish themselves as the elite of the new society. Many returned to Europe, finding the going too tough. Nonetheless, the trappings of success from Europe soon arrived in New Zealand—large houses, servants, balls, fine clothes, and etiquette.

It was not long before the British government conferred honors on residents of the colony, such as "Knights" and the female equivalent, "Dame." Now New Zealand has its own honors system—a reflection of the confidence New Zealanders have as a nation to stand apart from Great Britain.

Above and opposite: **New Zealanders enjoy one of the world's highest life expectancy rates—79.1 years for females and 73.4 years for males.**

European emigrants to New Zealand: a family with Dutch ancestry.

OTHER MIGRANTS

Migrants came also from Australia (mainly whalers and sealers, but also escaped convicts), France, Germany, Scandinavia, Dalmatia, Lebanon, southern Europe, and Asia. As with the Australians, some of the American whalers and sealers also decided to make New Zealand their base. The Chinese came out to work the gold fields of Central Otago in the 1860s and 1870s (as did many Australians), and a large influx of Dutch migrants poured into the country after World War II.

Nestling on the slopes of pristine pastureland by the calm waters of Banks Peninsula (near Christchurch) is the historic French settlement of Akaroa. French street names and stone buildings with shutters preserve its Gallic heritage. The main street, Rue Lavaud, commemorates French seaman Charles Lavaud, who captained the warship L'Aube that escorted Captain Jean Langlois's party of 63 emigrants from Rochefort in 1840. The Treaty of Waitangi and consequent British sovereignty over New Zealand ended Langlois's dreams of a French colony, but his settlers stayed on.

REFUGEES

New Zealand has one of the world's highest intakes of refugees per head of population. Refugees from Europe arrived in the 1930s and again after World War II. Many of these were Jews and Poles. Following the 1956 Hungarian uprising, there was an influx of refugees from Hungary.

The communist victory and takeover of South Vietnam also resulted in an exodus of refugees. Since 1975 about 7,000 Indochinese refugees have been resettled in New Zealand. Other refugees include Chileans, Russian Jews, East Europeans, and Assyrians, and more recently, Cambodians and Iraqis.

Somalians are among the many nationalities who have been attracted to the New Zealand lifestyle.

AN INTREPID EXPLORER

The topography of New Zealand made travel difficult for the early settlers. A young Englishman named Thomas Brunner set out on foot in 1846 to seek a pass across the Southern Alps. For 18 months, with the company of two Maori, he explored previously untrodden forested mountains. Often near to starvation, he subsisted on fern-roots and was reduced to eating his dog. He risked his life crossing dangerous rivers, and when his boots were finally torn to pieces his Maori companions made him sandals of flax and cabbage-tree leaves.

Before his great journey was over, Brunner fell ill (he lost the use of one leg) and while he was sheltering under an overhanging rock one night, all his precious sketches and notebooks that he kept in a flax basket fell into his campfire and were burned. But he did not lose heart and completed his successful expedition long after he had been given up for dead.

A New Zealander of British descent. For the early settlers there were no banana plantations (for New Zealand does not have a tropical climate) and life was hard going.

MOTHERLAND

Most New Zealanders are descendants of the early European settlers, notably from Britain. Until fairly recently, Britain was considered to be the motherland of most New Zealanders, with thousands of people making pilgrimages home to the "old country" every year. Today large numbers of people still visit Great Britain and Europe, but the purpose is more to gain overseas experience than to rediscover their ancestral roots.

TOUGH BEGINNINGS

Unlike early North American settlements, most New Zealand settlers did not come to New Zealand for political or religious reasons. Instead they came with the common goal of getting on in life—of owning and establishing their own farms and small businesses. This common purpose was to some extent reflected in the motto of the first New Zealand Coat of Arms, which read "Onward." But the land was not as fertile as the earlier settlers had been led to believe and much hard work was needed to clear thick bush before farms could be established.

PIONEERING SPIRIT

In adapting to their new environment, the early settlers had to make many compromises and improvisations. This has affected the way New Zealanders think of themselves today. "Kiwi ingenuity" is a common expression that epitomizes the positive attitude of New Zealanders to difficult or challenging situations, often involving the use of ordinary things to achieve extraordinary results. The stories of Richard Pearse, William Hamilton, and John Britten illustrate this New Zealand pioneering spirit.

Aviation Pioneer

Richard Pearse (1877–1953) was a Canterbury farmer who began the construction of his first aircraft in the late 19th century. He worked alone and without any financial backing. His aircraft had a bamboo and aluminum frame (made from flattened-out sheep-dip tins) braced with wire—a high-wing monoplane mounted on bicycle wheels with a span of about 26 feet (8 m). It was powered by a two-cylinder engine, which Pearse had built himself.

According to witnesses, he flew his aircraft for about 0.6 mile (1 km) on March 31, 1902, nearly two years before the famous Wright Brothers made their first flight in America. Unlike his American "brothers" however, Pearse did not go on to perfect his aircraft.

The First Jet Boat

William Hamilton (1899–1978) was a South Canterbury farmer and amateur engineer who developed and perfected the principle of water-jet propulsion to drive propellerless boats in the 1950s. By the 1960s there was a huge international demand for his commercial units. Hamilton's jet units are high-pressure water pumps driven by adapted car engines. Hamilton jet boats are now used on the Colorado River.

The Cardinal Britten Superbike

In little more than a garden shed the late John Britten, a Christchurch design engineer, toiled during the evenings to design and build the fastest four-stroke motorcycle in the world, the Cardinal Britten V1000. The revolutionary and innovative bike has aerodynamics unequaled by other motorcycles and breathtaking sleekness. At its widest point, the Britten's engine is no thicker than the rear tire.

Britten's achievement was quite remarkable. European and American motorcycle magazine writers heaped praise on the Britten V1000 bike after it won the International Battle of the Twins (two-cylinder bikes) at Assen, Holland in 1992.

For John Britten, designing bikes started as a hobby. He also wanted to prove "that there is room for the individual to compete against the multi-million dollar factory jobs." Now replicas of the Cardinal Brittens are being built for overseas collectors.

A laundry worker. Educated mainly in agriculture, metalworking, home management, and cookery, Maori migrants to the cities found work in the factories, the building trades, and laboring occupations.

TWO SOCIETIES—MAORI AND PAKEHA

With a predominance of Anglo-Saxons in the community, Maori people, who had been dominant in 1840, were subordinate to the Europeans by 1890. Two societies existed in New Zealand, although there was considerable racial interaction including some intermarriage between Maori and Europeans. Separate schools for Maori and Pakeha had the aim of preparing Maori for life among their own people and for Europeans to be trained in the professions, trade, and commerce. The Maori retained their traditional social structures and ceremonies such as the *hui* ("hoo-ee"), a political and a social gathering to which Europeans were often invited. Likewise, Europeans invited Maori chiefs to their balls and civic dinners.

By the early 1950s the Maori population had recovered substantially in numbers, but they had lost control of a significant portion of their land during the land wars of the late 19th century. There began a shift from the rural areas to the towns and cities, and by 1956 nearly a quarter of the Maori population were urban dwellers.

URBANIZATION OF MAORI

Various programs, including housing assistance, were established to help the Maori, especially the younger generation, to adapt to urban living and to integrate into mainstream Pakeha society. In the rural areas the Maori social structure follows the kinship networks of *whanau* ("FAA-no-oo"), or extended family, *hapu* ("huh-POO"), or sub-tribe, and *iwi* ("ee-wee"), or tribe. Within each tribe there is a clearly-defined system of rank and social control consisting of male and female elders, parents, uncles and aunts, religious mentors, and Maori wardens. When the Maori youth stepped out of these constraints— for instance by moving to the cities from their tribal location—many of them discovered they lacked the ability to manage their freedom and so they soon fell into conflict with the law. Sadly, even today there is a much higher proportion of Maori offenders in New Zealand prisons than Pakeha.

A serious attempt was made through the support of voluntary associations (including churches, culture, and sports clubs) to help the Maori retain their cultural identity and spiritual values. Central to rural Maori life is the *marae* ("mah-rye") with its ancestral house where both religious and secular activities take place. Eventually city *marae* were established and today there are even *marae* facilities on the campuses of secondary schools, colleges, and universities. However, for special occasions, such as a wedding, Maori people journey back to their traditional tribal areas, to the *marae* where their ancestors for generations debated important tribal decisions.

With the continuing urbanization of the Maori, intermarriage with the Pakeha increased. However, Maori people did not totally assimilate into the Pakeha culture, but instead took positive steps to maintain their own way of life.

MAORI ACTIVISTS

As they moved to the towns and cities, the Maori people learned much about the Pakeha political and social systems that governed their lives, and they began to use radical and activist means to gain equality and social justice and a return of their assets such as land and fisheries. Land became the symbol of Maori political subjection to Pakeha laws and was a sensitive issue in the central government.

Today the Maori people represent 13% of the total population of New Zealand and their cultural renaissance continues to strengthen. They have their own television program and many radio stations, which meet the needs of their communities. They now have a bigger representation in Parliament. An independent Maori Congress is a forum for tribes to come together to discuss important matters, and a Maori Council promotes the social and economic well-being of Maori and Maori culture. The Council has won several court cases over land claims against the New Zealand government.

MULTICULTURE

The second largest ethnic group in New Zealand is the Pacific Island Polynesians, who make up 3.5% of the total population and are based largely in the Auckland area. The Pacific Islanders have been flowing into New Zealand since the early 1960s, mainly for economic reasons. Young people from Pacific islands such as Western Samoa, Tonga, the Cook Islands, Niue, and Fiji have a greater potential of receiving a better education and finding employment in New Zealand than in their country or origin. A Ministry of Pacific Island Affairs ensures that the specific needs of the Pacific Islanders are met, for instance for skills training and employment placement service, while at the same time recognizing the cultural values and aspirations of the Islanders.

Since the 1980s an increasing number of Asian migrants have been coming to New Zealand. These include people from Taiwan, South Korea, Hong Kong, and mainland China.

AGING POPULATION

Compared with most developed Western countries, New Zealand has always had a young population because of the large-scale immigration of mainly young adults and a high birth rate in the 20th century. However, it has been predicted that New Zealand's population will grow more slowly in the future—by less than 1% a year, with the elderly population being the fastest growing age group.

New Zealand's elderly population will increase as the baby-boom generation (the large number of children born in the years after World War II) begin reaching retirement age after 2011.

LIFESTYLE

THERE USED TO BE A COMMONLY USED PHRASE among New Zealanders that described their basic attitude toward life—"She'll be right, mate." There is less complacency today, but there remains a sense of optimism. New Zealanders are positive about being New Zealanders.

FAMILY LIFE

Family life in New Zealand is changing. Although the traditional nuclear family still predominates, there are now de facto couple families, single parent families, and a few homosexual couple families. The divorce rate is increasing, but so too is the number of people remarrying. This often results in the blending of two families. Women are having children later in life. Many couples choose not to have children and those that do, have fewer: one-child families are now the most common.

Left and opposite: **Traditionally, Pakeha society has been a patriarchal one, but more and more women are contributing to the family finances. A very few (particularly if the husband is out of work or the wife is better qualified) are the main breadwinners. However, these circumstances tend to apply more to Maori and Pacific Island groups.**

A Maori family enjoy a picnic. For the matriarchal Maori society, the *whanau*, or extended family, may include three or four generations. Traditionally, the *whanau* provided shelter and food and cared for the land. It is still common to have members of the extended family living together in one household.

ON THE MARAE

The Maori believe a *marae* is their "standing place," a place where as a family they know they belong—in a sense their "home." The *marae* is a social place of hospitality where food and shelter are offered, but it is also a place of strict protocol. Women have a special role on the *marae*. Visitors assemble outside its gates and await the *karanga* ("kah-rah-ngah"), or call to enter, which is always made by a woman. A female leader returns the *karanga* on behalf of the visitors. She then leads the visitors in a slow procession onto the *marae*, calling as she goes.

Very important visitors to a *marae* are ceremonially challenged. Traditionally this was to establish whether visitors came in war or in peace. The challenger (always a man) makes fierce faces and noises, swinging a *taiaha* ("tye-aha"), or spear-like weapon, at the visitors to show that the warriors are ready to defend themselves if necessary. A small carved challenge dart is placed on the ground before the visitors and is always picked up by a male visitor. This indicates that the visitors arrive in peace.

Once visitors are in front of the meeting house, a *powhiri* ("POR-fi-ree"), or welcome, is given by elders, both men and women. The *powhiri* serves to ward off evil spirits, giving visitors safety as they move onto the *marae*. Those who take part in the *powhiri* are protected by the *tapu* ("tuh-poo") of the *marae*. *Tapu* is a purely Maori word associated with Maori spiritual beliefs and means "sacred" or "holy." When the Maori people declare something to be *tapu*, for example the ground on a *marae*, then it is necessary to approach this area according to prescribed ritual. Many Maori believe that to ignore *tapu* will bring sickness or even death.

After the welcome speeches are made, women sing a *waiata* ("wye-uh-tah"), or song. The last visitor to speak lays a *koha* ("kor-hah"), or gift, on the ground. Today the *koha* will often be money, but tribes used to give food. When all the speeches are over the visitors can greet the hosts with a *hongi* ("hor-ngee"). A *hongi* is a traditional greeting of Maori people. The pressing of noses during the *hongi* mingles the breath of two people in a show of unity.

The focal point of the *marae* is the meeting house, or *whare* ("fuh-re"), the shape of which is believed to represent the ancestor's body. A carved figure on the rooftop in front represents the head of the ancestor, while carved sloping pieces are the arms. Inside, a central ridge pole is the backbone and the rafters are the ribs. Large poles support the ridge pole and represent the link between the Sky Father and the Earth Mother.

EDUCATION

School is compulsory from age 6 to 16, but nearly all children begin school at 5 and many continue until age 18. The government partially funds an array of early childhood service providers, all of whom are independent of the government: these include play-centers, kindergartens, and Maori language "nests." After three years at secondary school most pupils take the School Certificate Examination. This can be in any number of subjects up to six and the student is credited with a grade for each subject. Many students stay in school for another one or two years, gaining higher qualifications to allow them to attend a university.

Private schools are partially funded by the government and charge student fees to cover their costs. Privately owned schools can also be integrated into the public system and receive funding. Integration has mostly been used by Catholic schools, some of which successfully serve the poorest areas in the cities. About 8% of school students attend integrated schools, and 3% private, fee-charging schools.

Educational achievement by Maori people has not kept pace with that of other groups, but alternate programs are being studied and tribes are given assistance to develop their own education plans. A limited number of schools that teach mainly in the Maori language are funded within the state system.

The Correspondence School is a world leader in distance education. It provides courses from early childhood to adult part-time students who wish to continue their basic education. Many students in isolated rural areas receive their education through the Correspondence School.

New Zealand has seven universities, with some 100,000 students. All the universities are publicly owned but run by independent councils. There are also some 25 publicly owned polytechnics that teach mostly lower-level courses, although some also issue degrees. Some 100,000 students attend the polytechnics. There are five colleges of education offering courses in teacher training. New Zealand secondary schools, polytechnics and universities accept many tuition paying foreign students.

University students celebrate graduation day. Universities and polytechnics are funded by the government on the basis of the number of students taking specified courses. Two Maori tertiary institutions are also funded by the government. The government also funds private providers of courses in priority areas.

Waiting for the bus.

THE WORKPLACE

There are now about as many women employed in the professions of law, medicine, and accounting as there are men. There is equal pay for equal work, but not always equal opportunity.

Many young people leave home around the age of 20 and live in apartments with their peers. This is often necessary in order to be near their place of work—particularly for those growing up in rural areas. Over half of those commuting to work go by car; less than 5% travel by bus or rail.

CITY LIFE

New Zealand cities are not places where heavy industry dominates the skyline. Modern high-rise office blocks specially designed to withstand earthquakes rub shoulders with sculptured buildings of interesting design and hundred-year-old pubs.

The area around Wellington, for example, has often been rocked by earthquakes; the city sits on a major earthquake fault line. Many of the city's older buildings have been replaced by buildings specially constructed to withstand severe quakes. As a result, Wellington boasts the most modern skyline of any city in New Zealand.

Auckland, Wellington, and Christchurch are cities of wide ethnic diversity and culture. This is evidenced in the huge variety of restaurants, street cafes, and colorful street-markets.

Shopping malls provide convenient one-stop shopping and places in which to stroll. Large supermarkets have displaced many small grocers, greengrocers, and butchers, but the local dairy continues. Usually managed by Indian families and open until late in the evenings, these small corner shops crammed with dairy products, ice-cream, cakes, confectionery, flowers, and magazines are still in demand.

Although inner city apartments are becoming popular, most city dwellers still reside in spacious houses with gardens in the surrounding suburbs. The economic divide is not as marked as, for example, that of New York, but the gap between the rich and the less-well-off is evident, particularly in parts of Auckland where there are large pockets of poorer Maori and Pacific Islanders.

Poorer neighborhoods in New Zealand are dominated by individual low-rise state housing. The facilities are adequate, although the neighborhoods are rougher and the schools less desirable.

Auckland is New Zealand's leading seaport, airport, and commercial and industrial center. The city is named after the first Earl of Auckland, George Eden, who was governor-general of India when the settlement of Auckland was founded.

65

RURAL LIFE

Life in the countryside and the small towns is community-driven. Entertainment is less passive than in the cities—country people have to create their own fun and they are very good at it. Social activities revolve around clubs, the local church, the local pub, and the *marae*.

The community hall is a focus for important birthdays such as a 21st, which is still celebrated in style. There are country balls, barn dances, musicals, and plays. And there are agricultural fairs, craft shows, flower shows, shearing competitions, and many other activities.

New Zealand farms are highly efficient. Unlike farmers in some other countries they are not heavily subsidized. There are 70,000 farms in New Zealand, the largest of which is 444,000 acres (180,000 hectares); the average size is 610 acres (250 hectares). Farms range from those raising livestock, such as sheep, dairy cattle, and deer to those involved in intensive horticulture, including wheat, oats, barley, maize, linseed, and potatoes.

Farmers also grow fodder crops to feed their herds. There are farms specializing in citrus fruit, kiwifruit, hops, tobacco, avocados, and many other fruits.

For those living in remote areas such as the high country sheep stations that nestle under the Southern Alps, the whole family is involved in tending the animals and crops. Children receive their education through the Correspondence School. Many go on to attend a boarding school in the cities for their secondary and vocational education. Not all young people return to work the family farm.

Helicopters are used extensively today to spray insecticides over crops, to drop poisons for noxious animals, and to bring fencing and other supplies into inaccessible country. There are more helicopters used in New Zealand per capita than anywhere else in the world.

FOOTROT FLATS

Murray Ball created "Footrot Flats" and its celebrated inhabitants, "Wal" and "Dog," in the mid-1970s. The famous cartoon strip is a self-mocking portrayal of a New Zealander character—hard-working and unassertive. The stories, involving a man, his dog, and sheep, have been translated into a successful stage musical, a cartoon feature film for the cinema, and many books.

Because it was found to be expensive and difficult to fertilize undulating or very hilly farmland by hand or from vehicles, in 1926, a Hunterville farmer, John Lambert, promoted the idea of using small planes from which to drop fertilizers. This has been claimed to be the first use of aerial top-dressing in the world.

If a couple is young, the bride's parents will usually finance the wedding. New Zealanders under the age of 20 require the consent of a parent or guardian before they can be legally married.

WEDDINGS

Many people choose to make their wedding vows and have their marriage blessed in a church (including Maori people, whose church is usually on the *marae*). Others have a simple ceremony in the office of a registrar. Contemporary young couples sometimes select a more unusual location, such as a snow-covered mountain top or a sandy beach.

Nowadays there is no set format for the wedding service—couples can decide for themselves how they want to express their vows to each other. Another break with tradition often occurs at the wedding reception following the service, when the bride chooses to be one of the speechmakers. Taking photographs is a very important part of the wedding and couples choose a variety of backgrounds, both unusual and traditional. After the photography session, the feast, cutting of the wedding cake, speeches, and often a dance, the newlyweds depart on their honeymoon. If the couple can afford it this might be a romantic holiday on a Pacific island.

FUNERALS

The Maori believe a body should not be left on its own after death. The family will usually collect it from the undertaker and place it on the *marae* where it can be watched over by relatives and friends until burial. To help relieve their emotional pain, Maori will often leave the coffin open so they can touch the body and weep over it. At the funeral service, speeches are made directly to the body in the belief that the spirit does not leave the presence of the body until the burial.

Some Pakeha also bring the body home from the undertaker for two or three days before burial. Others prefer to visit the body at the mortuary in the few days leading up to the funeral. A funeral service is usually held in a church of the deceased's religious denomination or in the undertaker's chapel. Hymns are sung, prayers are offered, and eulogies are given by relatives and close friends. The body is then either cremated or buried in a graveyard, which is usually just outside the town or city.

A Maori cemetery. For both Maori and Pakeha, a funeral involves the gathering of relatives and friends, many of whom travel long distances to pay their respects. This is an opportunity to celebrate the life of the deceased while sharing food after the funeral service.

S·LUKE

IN·MEMORY·OF
TAEKATA TOKOIHI

S·JOHN

IN·MEMORY·OF
TE ANIWARU KARAKA

RELIGION

CHRISTIANITY PLAYED A MAJOR PART in the early colonization of New Zealand. Before the white missionaries came in 1814, the Maori were a fiercely competitive tribal people with no written language. They worshiped their own gods and goddesses. Through their Christian teaching the missionaries encouraged the Maori people to live together peacefully and they transformed an intelligent but illiterate people into a literate society.

The main religion in New Zealand today is still Christianity. There are also Jehovah's Witnesses, Mormons, Hindus, Buddhists, and Jews. Unlike some European countries, such as Germany, no direct state aid is given to any form of religion.

MAORI MYTHOLOGY

Traditional Maori mythology gave meaning to the supernatural and to nature. The primal myth "Origins" tells of a supreme god, Io, who brought into being the heavens, the earth, and other gods, notably Io's Sky Father, Rangi, and Earth Mother, Papa, who produced 70 offspring, including man. Woman, however, was created by many gods.

Tane, god of the forests, shaped her body from clay and her eyes were set into pieces of clouds (to make the whites of her eyes); the god of winds gave her lungs and another god plucked feathers from birds to make hair. Tumatauenga, the god of war, arranged the muscles of her body and Rongo, the god of peace, gave her a stomach. Her spirit, blood, and power to breathe were supplied by Io.

Above: **Christchurch Cathedral—one of New Zealand's best-known churches.**

Opposite: **Church windows depict St. Luke and St. John.**

Above: **Engraving of Christ in a Maori coat.**

Opposite: **Richly decorated interior of a Maori church.**

Another myth tells of the demigod Maui, who hauled the North Island out of the sea with a chip of his grandmother's jawbone (claimed to have magical power) attached to his fishhook. Once his canoe was resting high and dry on the back of the "fish," Maui went off to make an offering to the gods.

While he was gone, his brothers, who had accompanied him on his fishing expedition, began to cut up the "fish" to eat it. This then is how the cliffs, valleys, plains, and mountain ranges of the North Island were formed.

THE WRITTEN WORD

The Protestant missionaries (Anglicans) were the first to arrive in New Zealand, and by 1819 they had established two mission stations in the Bay of Islands in the North Island. The Roman Catholics and Wesleyans (Methodists) arrived a few years later.

To reach out to the Maori, the Anglicans set up a printing press and began publishing portions of the Bible in Maori. These biblical texts became the textbook from which the Maori learned to read and write.

Maori people were quick to recognize the advantages of Christianity and literacy. There was also enhancement of *mana*, or prestige, to be gained by the tribal chiefs, who became patrons and protectors of missionaries, "the bearers of knowledge." Christianity spread very quickly among the Maori people, who became enthusiastic evangelists, often reaching new areas with the Bible ahead of the European missionaries.

LOST TRIBE OF ISRAEL?

Culturally, the Maori began to identify themselves with the Biblical stories. Through their appreciation of an oral history and the delineation of genealogies, or ancestral descent, some Maori supposedly "discovered" their genealogical roots in Judaism, calling themselves Hurai, or Jews. Until the Pakeha came, Maori people did not have a name for themselves, and it is thought that seeing themselves as a lost tribe of Israel gave some Maori a new sense of cultural identity.

A number of prophetic movements grew out of the new-found religion. Maori chiefs were inspired by Old Testament prophets and leaders, who were empowered by a God who communicated with them and helped them.

As more and more Maori became literate they began to interpret the Bible for themselves, and many forms of Maori Christianity emerged. Some forms retained the Maori notion of *tapu* with its associated rituals.

Toward the end of the 19th century, there was more uniformity within Maoridom. In a way, Christianity became a unifying force between Maori and Pakeha, but with the Maori very much subordinated.

THE RATANA MOVEMENT

Tahupotiki Ratana was an ordinary Maori with an unusual mission. He believed God called him to unify the Maori people as God's chosen race—identifying them with the Israelites as previous prophets had done. Bill Ratana, as he was known, rejected many traditional practices, such as tribalism and *tapu*, and encouraged practical pursuits such as wheat farming. He practiced faith healing all over the country. This was at a time—1918—when a major flu epidemic had seriously affected the Maori people. The population of the Maori was at an all-time low around the turn of the century, due, in large part, to their lack of resistance to European diseases.

Ratana's influence among the Maori increased, and in 1931, in a loose alliance with the Labor Party, the Ratana Church won its first Maori seat in Parliament, going on to strongly influence Maori national politics. Today, the Ratana Church is one of the fastest growing religions in New Zealand.

TARORE'S STORY

This is a true story. One day, Tarore and her people embarked on a long journey to avoid persecution by a rival tribe. They set out for a place of safety in Bay of Plenty on the North Island. On the way they camped overnight. As they settled down to sleep, the group were unaware that five raiders from a tribe in Rotorua were watching them.

In the early hours of the morning, the raiders stole many items from the camp. One warrior, called Uita, noticed Tarore was clutching a flax bag, which contained her precious copy of one of the books in the Bible. Tarore had been given a Maori translation of the Gospel of Luke by a missionary, following her attendance at a mission school where she had learned to read her language. Tarore refused to let go of her flax bag and Uita, determined to acquire it, thinking it must contain something valuable, killed her in the struggle.

When Uita and his group returned to Rotorua with their loot, they met a young man called Ripahau. Ripahau was able to read the Maori language and he read to them from Tarore's Gospel of Luke. The story told of how God reached down in love to his creation by sending His son Jesus Christ to bridge the gap between God and humankind. He read how Jesus healed the sick, preached a gospel of peace, sacrificed his life by dying on a cross to redeem everyone from their sins, and rose again to return to His heavenly father. The lives of all who listened were challenged and some were changed.

Ripahau himself became a Christian and a short while after he traveled to Kapiti Island, situated just off the southwest coast of the North Island. There he shared the word of God with Tamihana, the son of the great Maori chief Te Rauparaha, and also Tamihana's cousin. The cousins were so impressed with the words of Luke's Gospel they got into their canoes and traveled to the South Island where they spent 18 months sharing the gospel story. Many tribespeople converted to Christianity.

Young Tarore had died, but her little book had traveled on.

RELIGION TODAY

Although Christianity remains the main religion, an increasing number of New Zealanders claim to have no religion at all. Less than 20% of the population is actively involved in churches. Among the Christians in New Zealand, the Roman Catholics, Anglicans, Presbyterians, Pentecostals, and Baptists have the biggest percentage of followers. Other groups include Methodists, Lutherans, Brethren, the Salvation Army, Seventh Day Adventists, and Orthodox Christians.

Pentecostal churches are now the fastest growing. The Pentecostal church emerged from revivals in Wales and the United States in the early 20th century. During the 1960s and 1970s, a charismatic renewal movement swept through the mainstream churches, softening denominational barriers and bringing refreshing new worship music. New Pentecostal churches, with multicultural and youthful congregations, were founded during this time. Some churchgoers anticipate another revival.

Preparing for infant baptism. Centuries-old rituals are a very important part of religious observances in the more traditional churches.

The form of Christian church services ranges from the very traditional (found in some Roman Catholic and Anglican churches), with full choirs and organ accompaniment, chants, formal prayers, and ritualistic observances, to a freer, informal kind (enjoyed in the evangelical and Pentecostal churches), with contemporary music and spontaneous singing by the congregation.

A Christian radio station, pioneered 20 years ago in a shed in someone's backyard in Christchurch, now broadcasts seven days a week, 24 hours a day throughout the nation. It features lively, contemporary Christian music and bands from Australia, the United States, and New Zealand. As the first successful Christian radio network, it has been used as a model by other countries.

BREAKING DOWN BARRIERS

The first World Christian Gathering of Indigenous Peoples was held in Rotorua in 1996. Chaired by Monty Ohia, a prominent Maori educator, the conference drew together indigenous groups from around the globe, including American Indians, Australian Aborigines, and black South Africans.

A Maori gospel singer. In New Zealand, thousands gather annually at Christian "rock fests" to hear international and local Christian bands and artists.

The aim of the international conference was to build bridges between cultures and to encourage individual groups to retain their cultural distinctiveness within a Christian framework. Christianity has truly developed a long way from the early missionaries' view that to become fully Christianized, a people had to subordinate their own culture to that of the missionaries.

GOD'S OWN COUNTRY

Thomas Bracken, a 19th century English poet, was so impressed with the lavish beauty of New Zealand that he wrote a poem about it, calling it *God's Own Country*, often referred to now with a touch of irony as *Godzone*.

Bracken wrote another poem entitled *God Defend New Zealand*, which was set to music composed by John J. Woods and is now one of New Zealand's national anthems. *God Defend New Zealand* was given equal status with the traditional British anthem *God Save the Queen* in 1977 as a mark of New Zealand's identity.

The following are the first two of five verses of *God Defend New Zealand*, in English and Maori.

God Defend New Zealand

God of nations at Thy feet
In the bonds of love we meet.
Hear our voices, we entreat,
God defend our free land.
Guard Pacific's triple star
From the shafts of strife and war,
Make her praises heard afar,
God defend New Zealand.

Men of every creed and race
Gather here before Thy face,
Asking Thee to bless this place,
God defend our free land.
From dissension, envy, hate,
And corruption, guard our state,
Make our country good and great,
God defend New Zealand.

Aotearoa

*E Ihoa Atua,
O nga Iwi! Matoura,
Ata whakarongona;
Me aroha roa.
Kia hua ko te pai;
Kia tau to atawhai;
Manaakitia mai
Aotearoa.*

*Ona mano tangata
Kiri whereo, kiri ma,
Iwi Maori Pakeha
Repeke katoa,
Nei ka tono ko nga he
Mau e whakaahu ke,
Kia ora marire
Aotearoa.*

TODAY'S MISSIONS

New Zealand has the highest number of missionaries per capita in the Western world. As a nation, people give generously to charitable causes such as World Vision and Feed the Hungry. Food banks run by volunteers and many other missions of compassion minister to the needy.

PUTIPUTI RA
ORGANIC TRADERS

ORGANIC PRODUCE

SUPPLEMENTS

GREEN CLEANING &
HAIRCARE PRODUCTS

WHOLE FOODS

DRIED FRUIT

ORGANIC
BEVERAGES
DAIRY PRODUCTS

the AMAZON CAFE

...PRODUCE
...LEMENTS
...CLEANING
...PRODUCTS

ORGA...
TRADER...
PH. 430 0606

BIN INN

BULK
FOOD
MARKET

the
AMAZON
CAFE

Vegetarian
and
Wholefood Cafe

Purolator
products

...RK PL...
...ROM U.S....

...HE ORIGINAL
...OIL FILTER

AUTOMO...

LANGUAGE

ENGLISH, THE OFFICIAL LANGUAGE of New Zealand, was inherited from the early British colonizers. English is the first language of about 95% of the population and the only language spoken by some 90%, making New Zealand one of the most monolingual nations in the world.

Since 1987 Maori has also become an official language. After years of decline, there is now renewed interest, especially among the young, both Maori and non-Maori.

NEW ZEALAND GRAMMAR

People in New Zealand are educated in Standard British English. In fact, New Zealand English is more like British English than any other non-European variety. The national newspapers and public documents are written in Standard English. Nevertheless, Maori words have found their way into the vocabulary, and the language has been influenced by both Australian and American English.

When they are overseas, New Zealanders are often mistaken for Australians, but to a New Zealand ear the Australian accent sounds quite different—just as a Canadian accent is noticeable to an American. The main difference concerns the short "i" vowel. Australian "fish and chips" sounds like *feesh and cheeps* to a New Zealander, who would pronounce it *fush and chups*, and "Sydney" sounds like *Seedney*.

However, the practice of turning a statement into what seems a question—what phonetic experts call high rising terminal intonation—is common to both.

Above: **A young couple make a telephone call.**

Opposite: **Bright signs and simple messages in English, with just a touch of Maori.**

How different is New Zealand English from, say, American English? English-speaking tourists in New Zealand have found it helpful to carry a New Zealand English dictionary or a book of common expressions to understand the English spoken there.

PRONUNCIATION

New Zealand pronunciation departs from Standard British English in the intonation of vowel sounds, particularly in closing diphthongs. For example, "today" sounds like *todie*; "high" sounds like *hoi*, "hello" sounds like *helleouw*, and "trout" sounds like *treout*. Another common trait is the centralized "i" producing *ut* for "it" and *paintud* for "painted." Since the early 1960s, the distinction of vowel sounds in words like ear and air, here and hair, and beer and bare have become less pronounced.

PECULIARITIES

There are many compounded words, new meanings, and colloquial expressions in the language that derive from a specifically New Zealand experience and environment. Examples are *cow-cockie* (dairy farmer); *section* (plot of land); and *up the boohai* (*boohai* is a remote district or area; *up the boohai* means "very much awry").

A NEW ZEALAND GLOSSARY

amber	beer
arvo	afternoon
backbone of the country	the farming community
beaut	something or someone of excellent quality
chocker	filled to capacity
clobbering machine	pressure by fellow New Zealanders not to be seen as too successful
cobber	a mate (friend)
dill	someone who behaves stupidly
dinky-die	truly, absolutely ("I did win the game, dinky-die!")
footie	rugby union or league football
gidday	a common greeting
good on you	a term of encouragement
hard case	an entertaining or self-reliant person
hooray	a Kiwi farewell
joker	a bloke (Kiwi man)
kia ora ("kev-ah aw-rah")	good luck! (a Maori greeting)
kiwi	a New Zealander (after the native bird)
mainland	the South Island
mate	a friend, but also used as an informal (and presumptuous) greeting to a visitor
mingie	stingy ("don't be mingie!")
ordinary bloke, ordinary joker	a sensible Kiwi male having a humble opinion of himself
shout	to treat ("I'll shout you a meal")
sport	a way of addressing someone ("Howya sport?")
throw a wobbly	an overdisplay of emotion, usually anger
within coo-ee of	"not to come within coo-ee of" means to fall grossly short of reaching a goal
wop-wops	"he lives in the wop-wops" means he lives in a very remote area

MAORI LANGUAGE

New Zealand Maori is a Polynesian language closely related to Cook Islands Maori, Tahitian, and Hawaiian. It is the first language of some 50,000 adult Maori New Zealanders (12% of the Maori population). One of the most important aspects of the Maori renaissance of the 1970s was the renewal of interest by the Maori in their indigenous language. There are more speakers of Maori now than at the beginning of the 20th century.

Use of the Maori language was encouraged through a Maori-language preschool movement and by Maori-language immersion primary schools. The former is a *whanau,* or extended family base, where very young children are taught traditional knowledge, crafts, and customs through the medium of Maori language. The Maori-language immersion primary schools teach pupils the entire school curriculum in Maori. Thousands of secondary school pupils also take Maori language as a subject.

A Maori Language Commission assists government departments and other Crown agencies in offering a range of services in Maori.

MISSIONARIES GIVE LITERACY

When the first missionaries arrived in New Zealand the Maori did not have a written form of language. Their genealogies were recorded in the stylized figures carved on the wooden poles of their ancestral meeting houses, while folk art related their myths and legends. Then, in 1820, two Anglican missionaries traveled back to England, taking with them two important Maori chiefs. At Cambridge University, England, they produced the first Maori grammar.

This important work was further developed during the next decade by the missionaries. The Maori people were so eager to learn they would use gunpowder instead of chalk when the latter was not available to them. By the mid-1830s Maori who wished to be held in high regard recognized the need to be literate.

Maori epitaph on a tombstone. By the 1840s there were proportionately more Maori literate in Maori than English people literate in English in New Zealand.

Choral notes in Maori. A survey disclosed that almost 60% of all schoolchildren in New Zealand, Maori and non-Maori, now study the language.

A LIVING LANGUAGE

Language is always changing, and the Maori were quick to extend their vocabulary to take account of foreign ideas and objects. Maori people began to fit foreign words to their own phonology. For example, *Hune* ("HOO-ne") is June, *moni* ("mor-nee") is money, and *hipi* ("hip-ee") is sheep.

Today Maori speakers like to adapt Maori words and phrases to express new ideas and objects. Maori vocabulary has also found its way into New Zealand English. Most of these borrowed words are proper nouns, for example, bird names such as kiwi and kakapo; plant names such as manuka and *kumara*; and trees such as kauri and rimu. Other Maori words add a richness of expression, such as *mana*—used to connote a person's prestige, status, or honor. *Mana* is a very important concept in Maoridom.

There are very many places with Maori names including mountains, rivers, and lakes—some of which have an English name as well, for example, Mount Taranaki is Mount Egmont. In tourist centers such as Rotorua and Queenstown, public information signs are displayed in several languages.

MAORI PRONUNCIATION

Every syllable in Maori should be pronounced clearly and must end with a vowel. Practice sounding the syllables separately at first, then run them together. For example, Maa-or-ri, Maori. There are five vowel sounds, each of which may be said short or long. The vowels sound like the following:

short *a*, like *u* in "hut"
long *aa*, like *a* in "Chicago"
short *i*, like *i* in "hit"
long *ii*, like *ee* in "keep"
short *e*, like *e* in "fleck"

long *ee*, like *ai* in "fair"
short *o*, like *or* in "distort"
long *oo*, like *ore* in "sore"
short *u*, like *u* in "put"
long *uu*, like *oo* in "spoon"

Any pair of different vowels is called a diphthong. Maori diphthongs retain the sound of the second vowel quite clearly and most of them are not matched in sound by anything in English, for example, *ae*, sounds like *igh* in "high."

Consonants are sounded as they are in English, with the exception of *wh*, which sounds more like *f*, and *ng*, which always sounds like the *ng* in the nasal-sounding "clanger" rather than "linger."

ARTS

THROUGH THE ARTS, NEW ZEALANDERS have both sought after and found expression for their cultural identity. As they gradually shifted their focus away from Britain and Europe for their source of cultural identity, they have begun to see themselves as part of the Asia Pacific and an appreciation of the different colors within their own society has grown. National identity is founded less on New Zealand being different from other countries and more on the differences found within. Now there is one sound, but many voices.

MAORI ART

Art in New Zealand had its origins in Maori culture centuries before European settlement. While the men carved complex images out of wood, stone, and bone, the women crafted flax fiber into clothing, mats, and baskets.

Maori women were taught the ritualistic art of weaving. They wove mostly cloaks—feather-decorated, for mourning, ceremonial dog-skin cloaks, and a closely woven cloak designed to ward off spears in battle.

Opposite: **New Zealanders spend their lunch break beside a huge wall mural.**

Left: **A Maori sculptor at work.**

Women were expert in *tukutuku* ("took-oo-took-oo"), the art of creating symbolic geometric designs using light, colored swamp reeds skillfully attached with flax cord to horizontal laths. *Tukutuku* panels make a striking contrast to the carved ancestral figures on the walls of Maori meeting houses.

Carvers, trained in their youth by priestly experts, were given high status in traditional Maori culture. The carvings usually symbolized the veneration of ancestors and appeared not only in ancestral meeting houses but decorated their storehouses and war canoes as well. A characteristic motif incorporated in the carving was the single and double spiral. On ceremonial occasions and in times of war, warriors painted colorful patterns on their face and body. Coloring materials (usually mixed with shark oil) included white clay, charcoal, and red ochre. Red was regarded as a sacred color.

Tattooing of the body was a ritualized art also performed by priestly experts. Spiraled designs were incised with bone and jade chisels tapped with a rod, and colored with blue pigment. Each person's *moko* ("morkor"), or tattoo, was different and was a form of identification. The performing priest's own body was considered too sacred to tattoo. Instead his body designs were painted with colors derived from plants and ochre. Today tattoos are still performed by experts, but using modern equipment.

EUROPEAN ART

The first European style of art expressed in New Zealand were the pen drawings recording the impressions of the country by the draftsmen accompanying the exploratory expeditions. Then came visiting artists from Europe eager to paint Maori activities and artifacts, followed by British artists in the early colonial period who painted to promote the country back home in England.

Charles Goldie, one of New Zealand's best known artists, is famous for his Maori portraits. Painting in the early years of the 20th century and at a time when the Maori population was thought to be dying out, his detailed portraits are of considerable historical interest and are highly valued.

In the paintings of early artists, nature was portrayed as an overwhelming, dominant force. But as the land was cleared and cultivated by the early colonists, landscapes began to take on a different aspect. Frances Hodgkins is the most internationally celebrated painter, known for her still-life and landscape paintings. However, much of her painting was done in England, where she spent most of her life in the early part of the 20th century.

Rita Angus helped give New Zealand painting a sense of its own direction during the 1930s and 1940s. Her landscapes captured the distinctive color of New Zealand with its sharp light. The late Colin McCahon is the most important contemporary artist. He integrated into his landscape paintings in the 1970s and 1980s spiritual words and phrases, with powerful effect.

Nineteenth-century church architecture in Dunedin. A distinct New Zealand style in architecture, sculpture, pottery, and wood turning, based on a blend of European, Maori, and Asia-Pacific themes and influences has since developed.

LITERATURE

Women in New Zealand have been closely involved with the arts since colonial times. In contrast with other professions, literature and the arts are more loosely structured, giving freedom to women to attain higher prominence and success.

Katherine Mansfield (1888–1923) is New Zealand's most distinguished author. Born in Wellington, her real name was Kathleen Beauchamp. She went to London at the age of 14 to finish her education, then returned to New Zealand for two years. At 19, Katherine went back to London where she associated with innovative writers, such as Virginia Woolf, T.S. Eliot, and D.H. Lawrence.

Although she spent her short adult life in Europe (she died at the age of 34 from tuberculosis), many of Mansfield's stories draw on her memory of a New Zealand childhood. Her short stories, such as *Prelude* (published 1918), *At the Bay*, *The Garden Party*, and many others, have earned her the reputation as one of the finest short story writers in English. D.H. Lawrence compared her to Dickens. Her writing is considered to be both poetic and powerful.

Katherine Mansfield— Virginia Woolf once said of her: "I was jealous of her writing. The only writing I have ever been jealous of."

Another writer, Dame Ngaio Marsh (1899–1982), became an internationally known writer of detective stories, completing more than 30 whodunnits.

New Zealand's most gifted novelist, Janet Frame (born 1924), came to be recognized internationally in 1957 with the publication of *Owls Do Cry*. Her autobiographical trilogy—*To the Island* (1983), *An Angel at My Table*

90

(1984), and *The Envoy from Mirror City* (1985) were later published in one volume as *An Angel at My Table*, and an acclaimed television film was made under this title by New Zealand director Jane Campion.

Keri Hulme (born 1947), a novelist, short story writer, and poet with Maori origins, won the prestigious Booker McConnell Prize for fiction in 1985 for her novel *The Bone People* (1983). Interestingly, her novel, steeped in Maori mythology, was first produced in book form by a Maori women's collective and became a New Zealand bestseller through word of mouth. Subsequently, an international publisher ensured a worldwide audience.

Some contemporary leading writers for adults have also written for children, such as Joy Cowley, Patricia Grace, and Maurice Gee. In earlier years young people growing up in New Zealand read stories and fairy tales from British and European cultures. Now these and other authors have given New Zealand children stories set in their own culture to which they can relate. Margaret Mahy is New Zealand's best-known writer for children and has twice won the Carnegie Medal (the top international award for children's literature) for her works, *The Haunting* and *The Changeover*.

Award-winning writer Keri Hulme, another prominent New Zealander.

James K. Baxter (1926–72) is widely regarded as the most gifted poet New Zealand has produced. He had no regard for materialistic values and in the 1960s he became a controversial figure, setting up a commune for those who felt they did not fit within New Zealand society, both Maori and Pakeha. His verse is considered to be both profound and beautiful.

A symphony in the park.

MUSIC

There is a strong tradition of music in New Zealand—especially choral singing, which has been enriched by the singing traditions of the Maori and Pacific Islanders. At a local level many people love to perform in musicals, choirs, orchestras, ensembles, and bands of all kinds, including brass bands and Scottish pipe bands.

The New Zealand Symphony Orchestra (NZSO) based in Wellington spends much of its time traveling throughout the country, making the music of international and national composers accessible to everyone. It regularly attracts world-famous soloists and conductors and makes recordings for several major international labels. In addition to the national orchestra, there are prominent regional orchestras, a highly-acclaimed New Zealand Chamber Orchestra, and a national brass band.

DOUGLAS LILBURN

Douglas Lilburn (born 1915) is a prolific contemporary composer. His published and recorded works include symphonies, songs, and piano and guitar pieces. Eager to present a distinctive New Zealand voice, Lilburn has drawn inspiration from the natural environment: the light, sounds, colors, and shapes that make up the landscapes and seascapes. This is reflected in some of the names of his compositions, for example, *Aotearoa Overture*, *Landfall in Unknown Seas*, *A Song of Islands*, and *Soundscape with Lake and River* (the latter is an electronic work).

By his example as composer and his teachings, Lilburn has encouraged young composers to create a music tradition of their own. One of his best known works is the song cycle *Sings Harry*, set to Dennis Glover's poem about a romantic, tough, back-country character.

MAORI SONG AND DANCE

The traditional Maori song of welcome, the *waiata*, is still alive today in Maoridom. But around the turn of the century a new form of Maori music emerged, the "action song." In a way, the Maori action song has become the national dance of New Zealand. Maori concert groups perform action songs for tourists and also travel overseas. Sometimes these songs use melodies from other countries, such as *Blue Eyes*, the waltz tune behind *E Pari Ra*, a tribute and lament for Maori soldiers of World War I. A Maori woman combined action song with electroacoustic dance rhythms to create an international hit, *Poi-e*.

According to Maori legend, the wide, bulging eyes seen on the carved figures inside the traditional meeting houses represent the eyes of the owl—seen as a wise bird. When Rongo, the god of peace, built a sacred house of learning, an owl was buried beneath it for protection against evil. It is said too that the glaring eyes of the carved figures mimic the owl glaring at the fantail (a small native bird with a tail shaped like a fan) when it annoys him with its constant and energetic flitting. Maori performers of action songs and *haka* ("huh-kuh") imitate both birds: the men by making their eyes look fierce during the *haka* and the women by swinging their *poi* ("poy"), or small balls on the end of a string, in movements that resemble the flight of the fantail.

The *haka* is an energetic, aggressive action song, more like a chanting war dance and traditionally performed by men. Today it is commonly used by rugby teams, notably the touring All Blacks, for performance on the field immediately before a match.

Through the action song, Maori people are able to express the vitality and freshness of their own unique culture.

Opposite: **New Zealand-born actor Sam Neil has appeared in numerous Hollywood movies.**

OPERA

There are professional opera companies based in Auckland, Wellington, and Christchurch, each presenting two or three productions a year. Internationally acclaimed opera and concert singers include Patrick Power, Christopher Doig, Dame Malvina Major, Patricia Payne, Heather Begg, Keith Lewis, and Donald McIntyre. However, New Zealand's most famous opera singer is Gisborne-born Kiri Te Kanawa. In 1982 she was made a Dame Commander of the Order of the British Empire.

KIRI TE KANAWA

Dame Kiri Te Kanawa (born 1944) is one of the world's leading operatic sopranos. She was educated at St. Mary's College, Auckland, where she studied singing with Sister Mary Leo from 1959 to 1965, when she won the New Zealand Mobil Song Quest and the *Melbourne Sun* aria competition. The following year she was awarded an arts council scholarship to study singing in London. She soon became an international star and is now sought after by the world's leading opera companies.

Te Kanawa delighted television audiences around the world when she sang at the royal wedding of Prince Charles and Princess Diana. Although she has been based in London for the past 30 years, she periodically returns to her homeland where she attracts very large audiences and much adulation.

MOVIES

Going to the movies is a favorite pastime of New Zealanders, and New Zealand's feature film, television, and commercial production industries are applauded worldwide.

Perhaps New Zealand's best known movie-maker is Jane Campion, who was born in Wellington in 1954. Campion has established herself as a top movie director, gaining worldwide recognition for *The Piano*, which she wrote and directed. This 1993 Academy Award-winning movie is an evocative portrayal of early colonial life on the South Island's West Coast. Among the movie's actors and actresses are New Zealanders Sam Neil and Anna Paquin.

In many ways Anna Paquin is just an ordinary 14-year-old girl attending an all-girls school in Wellington. But she has already achieved what Hollywood stars dream about. She won an Oscar—the second youngest person to do so—when she took the Best Supporting Actress Award for her enchanting performance in *The Piano* (in which she had more lines than anyone else in the movie).

Her response to winning the Oscar? "It's pretty cool." Anna has gone on to star in *Jane Eyre, Fly Away Home*, and *The Member of the Wedding*.

LEISURE

SPORTS PLAY AN IMPORTANT PART IN SHAPING New Zealand's national image. Achieving against all odds, overcoming hurdles and difficulties, and facing a challenge head-on are all prized qualities, both on and off the playing field. New Zealand mountaineer Sir Edmund Hillary, who in 1953 became the first man in the world (with Sherpa Tensing Norgay) to reach the summit of Mount Everest, is a prime example of this conquering spirit.

Competitive sporting activities are part of the compulsory education system. The international caliber of New Zealand's sports people has contributed much to the cultural identity of New Zealand. Government policy ensures that sports, fitness, and leisure activities are available to all who wish to participate, including people with disabilities. The Hillary Commission for Sport, Fitness, and Leisure is a public funding agency for most of New Zealand's sporting and leisure activities.

In 1958 Sir Edmund Hillary became the first man to drive overland to the South Pole. He did so in specially adapted New Zealand farm tractors. Hillary is now featured on the New Zealand five-dollar note.

Opposite: **The bungee jump—a leap of faith invented by a New Zealander that has gained worldwide popularity.**

Left: **Father and daughter show off their catch. New Zealand has many fishing spots for enthusiasts.**

Young rugby players at an international youth tournament. There are about 600 rugby clubs throughout the country and it is the dream of many young players to one day wear the black jersey of the New Zealand national team.

COMPETITIVE SPORTS

Rugby union is the national sport, with the internationally renowned All Blacks starring as a symbol of national identity. The first World Cup Rugby competition in 1987 was won by the All Blacks, who remained unbeaten for four years. The All Blacks do not derive their name from race (the team contains the best New Zealand players, regardless of ethnicity), but from the color of their outfit—black jersey and pants.

In fact, much effort has been made to try and keep politics out of the sporting arena. However, in 1981 an exclusively all-white Springbok team from South Africa toured New Zealand. This upset many New Zealanders and caused unprecedented protests.

Cricket has been played in New Zealand for over 150 years and is New Zealand's oldest organized sport. There are both men's and women's teams. New Zealand secured its first test win against the West Indies in 1956 and its first test series (against Pakistan) in 1969. Since then, New Zealand has had particular success in international one-day matches, which are very popular with television viewers. The introduction of one-day cricket has resulted in greater participation in the sport; it is now New Zealand's fastest growing sport at the junior level. Sir Richard Hadlee was one of the sport's outstanding players. He retired in 1990 with the world record for wickets taken in test matches—431. He was also a superb fast bowler and one of the world's best allround players.

International success has also been achieved in track and field athletics, netball, squash, softball, golf, equestrian events, boxing, ice racing, skiing, and water sports such as yachting, rowing, windsurfing, and swimming.

THE AMERICA'S CUP

In 1993/94, New Zealand yachts won the Whitbread round-the-world race. National fervor was aroused again in 1995 when New Zealand's yacht *Black Magic*, crewed by Team New Zealand, won the prestigious America's Cup. Joyous celebrations followed.

Intense international interest has been shown not only in the design and special capabilities of the yachts, but also in the first real-time 3D computer animation package designed in New Zealand to relay the 1992 America's Cup race. Preparations are now being made to host the next America's Cup yacht race in New Zealand in 1999.

Susan Devoy, the greatest squash player New Zealand has produced, dominated the women's game internationally from the second half of the 1980s to the early 1990s. In 1984, at age 20, she became the youngest ever top-ranked player in the world. She lost her world title in 1989, but beat the new world champion a few weeks later to take the English Open for the sixth successive year.

New Zealand sports people are always eager participants in both the Olympic and Commonwealth Games, and the ratio of medals won per thousand of population is often high. The 1990 Commonwealth Games held in Auckland attracted the biggest number of participants to date. A prominent sports personality is Arthur Lydiard, a marathon runner who later trained young athletes, notably the successful New Zealand Olympic runners Peter Snell and Murray Halberg.

A swimming hole near Whangarei Falls draws a crowd.

LEISURE SPORTS

Fitness is an important element of the New Zealand lifestyle, with about half the population belonging to a sports, fitness, or leisure club. It is not unusual in the cities at lunchtime to see office workers jogging around the streets, parks, and waterfronts. The most popular sports are swimming, cycling, snooker/pool, tennis, and aerobics. Golf is popular with middle-aged people, while the older age group plays bowls. People engage in these activities not only to keep fit and healthy but to enjoy the company of others.

THE GREAT OUTDOORS

New Zealanders love the great outdoors. They are blessed with a country possessing great variety and natural beauty. Many people like to walk the peaceful tracks in the national parks and reserves, such as the 34 mile (55 km) Milford Track in Fjordland, where they can appreciate the native flora

and fauna, experience cascading waterfalls, and listen to the songs of unusual birds. Others prefer rock climbing, mountain climbing, or mountain biking. The warm waters of the east coast of the North Island provide some of the best surf, line, and spear fishing in the world, and big game hunting offers deer, chamois, tahr, wild pigs, goats, and wallaby.

Father and daughters set out on a short bush walk. No city or town is far from rivers, lakes, forests, mountains, or sea. The environment is clean and the scenery often spectacular.

GOING BUSH

It is possible to enjoy adventures well away from civilization in New Zealand—to be able to tramp for days in alpine isolation and rough it in the back-country bush. There are a few who spend most of their lives tramping and camping in splendid solitude. One such person was the late Barry Crump, who now appears on one of the country's postage stamps wearing the bushman's national costume—a "swandry" (very thick woolen checked overshirt), waterproof hat, and heavy-duty boots. Crump wrote a number of humorous novels, his best and most famous being *A Good Keen Man.*

HOLIDAYS

Going on holiday is part of the Kiwi lifestyle. Usually, holidays are taken during the summer months, mainly in January, though many will include winter breaks to the ski-fields. Families flock to camping grounds near the sea or the lakes where they can fish, swim, water-ski, canoe, or sail their yachts. Some of the faster flowing rivers are ideal for white-water rafting, while others are great for jet boat rides. Many people stay in the family "bach." The bach, or small cottage, often set in fairly remote areas and containing the barest essentials, offers relaxed and simple living.

The weekend retreat to the bach or a place in a rural area is popular with those who live demanding or very busy lives. It is a chance to explore the countryside, perhaps on horseback or in tough, four-wheel-drive vehicles. The more adventurous enjoy hang-gliding, parachute-jumping, or deep-sea diving.

When they are not making the most of their clean, green environment, New Zealanders love to read. In fact it is estimated they read and buy more books per head of population than any other English-speaking country.

HOMES AND GARDENS

Family life centers around the home. Houses range in style from late 19th century cottages to very modern individually designed homes. Regional and climatic differences influenced the way the early settlers housed themselves. The large-windowed timber houses with their open verandahs in Northland contrast with the stone buildings with their smaller windows in Southland where the climate is much cooler.

In the winter months, visitors from around the world join New Zealanders on the many excellent ski-fields in both the North and South Islands. The skiing season runs from June to late October.

Today there is more emphasis on indoor/outdoor living styles with wide glass doors opening directly onto balconies, patios, or gardens. Apart from the comparatively few inner city apartment blocks, each house is detached, sitting on its own land. Many have two stories, while some have their own swimming pools and tennis courts. Noticeable, however, is the shift away from small houses on large plots to large houses on smaller plots. It is still the aim of the majority of New Zealanders to own their own home. About 74% of them do, which is higher than many other Western countries (66% for the United Kingdom, 64% for the United States, and 62% for Canada). As a nation of "do-it-yourselfers," New Zealanders devote a lot of energy and leisure-time to home improvements.

Gardening is a favorite hobby for thousands of New Zealanders. There are cottage gardens, wild gardens, formal gardens, herb gardens, native plant gardens, exotic gardens, and specialist gardens. Flower shows and television and radio programs keep keen gardeners up-to-date with the latest techniques and hybrids.

FESTIVALS

NEW ZEALAND'S NATIONAL HOLIDAYS include New Year's Day, Waitangi Day, Easter, ANZAC Day, the Queen's Birthday, Labor Day, and Christmas. Waitangi Day and ANZAC Day are particularly significant as they mark turning points in the nation's history.

But festival fun is not confined to national holidays. Throughout the year and around the country, the events calendar is crowded with a great many activities, such as country music festivals, hot-air balloon fiestas, movie festivals, air pageants, opera festivals, rock fests, jazz and blues fests, fashion competitions, spring blossom festivals, and art and craft shows.

New Zealand's wide cultural mix is celebrated in Chinese dragon boat races, Welsh choral singing festivals, Japanese festivals, Irish and Scottish cultural festivals, and Asia Pacific and Maori performing arts festivals. Queenstown's winter festival is a week of entertainment and revelry.

"A new generation is having to deal with difficult questions of nationhood. ... Today we grapple with the demands of expressing that sense of shared nationhood in a manner that is fair and just. ... By doing so we will truly honor those who fought for peace on foreign fields in our name."

—*Prime Minister Jim Bolger, addressing ANZAC Day service, 1997*

Opposite: **Participants in colorful costumes at a Wellington street festival.**

Left: **A veteran remembers his fallen colleagues on ANZAC Day.**

Overleaf: **Waitangi Day jet display.**

WAITANGI DAY

Every year on February 6, a celebration takes place to commemorate the signing of the Treaty of Waitangi in 1840. Maori tribal leaders and many others join the governor-general, the prime minister, and leading dignitaries in a formal ceremony on the grounds of the Treaty House at Waitangi.

It is a time for New Zealanders, in particular the Maori and Pakeha, to reflect on their past, to appreciate the progress that has been made in the unifying of two peoples, and to consider the way forward in the future. Waitangi Day focuses attention on the implications of the founding document of the nation.

Over the years the government has met numerous claims by Maori tribes. Nevertheless, there is still more to be achieved for the Maori and Waitangi Day celebrations are traditionally peppered with Maori protesters. For the first time, in 1997, the official Waitangi Day ceremony took place at the governor-general's residence in Wellington—leaving Maori protesters to themselves in Waitangi. This has led to considerations about changing the public holiday from Waitangi Day to New Zealand Day, to shift attention away from grievances and refocus on New Zealand as a multicultural nation.

ANZAC DAY

ANZAC stands for the Australian and New Zealand Army Corps, which was formed during World War I. On April 25, 1915, at dawn, the ANZACs landed on the beach of Gallipoli in Turkey, which was held by the Turks. They fought gallantly a campaign planned by British politicians and led by British officers. Thousands of lives were lost and so was the campaign.

But the courage of the ANZACs in what was an impossible situation led to a celebration of the landing when the war was over. The returned soldiers paraded through the streets of London to receive honor from the king and queen outside Buckingham Palace. It marked the beginning of a new "mateship" between the Australians and New Zealanders, and today the word "ANZAC" is often used to describe a combination of effort between the two countries.

ANZAC Day parade.

FREYBERG—FROM DENTIST TO GENERAL AND BEYOND

A young dentist working in rural New Zealand called Bernard Freyberg joined the British Navy at the beginning of World War I. At Gallipoli, he distracted the attention of the Turks from the main landing by swimming ashore to a separate beach where he came under heavy fire. His exploits became legendary, and while serving in France, he was awarded numerous medals for courage, including the highest honor, the Victoria Cross. He was wounded nine times and finished the war as a brigadier general.

During World War II, Freyberg commanded the New Zealand troops in the Middle East. In 1942 he was again wounded and again decorated for bravery. After the war, the by now Lord Freyberg was governor-general of New Zealand for six years. In Britain the queen presented him the high, honorary position of Lieutenant Governor of Windsor Castle.

ANZAC Day is a time for New Zealanders to remember and honor their soldiers and heroes from all wars. The day starts with dawn parades throughout the country. Old soldiers proudly wearing their medals march behind military and other brass bands to a central point of commemoration —usually a cenotaph on which is inscribed the names of the fallen soldiers from the locality.

Many civilians, both young and old, join them. Traditionally the ANZAC service includes a trumpet fanfare, *The Last Post*. Wreaths are laid, hymns are sung, and speeches are made. A national service is held in Wellington, presided over by leading officials representing the military, government, diplomats, and the church.

Veterans with their war medals. There are only two surviving New Zealand ANZACs from 1915: both are 100 years old.

CHRISTMAS

Christmas festivities in New Zealand begin about the middle of November with colorful street parades and brightly decorated shops. Although Christmas time is summertime in New Zealand, Santa Claus still arrives in a reindeer-driven sleigh, warmly dressed in his Nordic costume! Little children clamber onto his knee in the department stores and shopping malls to request toys and presents. Many of the traditions of the northern hemisphere are followed, including the preparation and baking of large Christmas fruitcakes and mince pies.

Gifts are exchanged on Christmas Day, which is traditionally the time when extended families get together to celebrate the festive season. Young children get up very early to see if Santa Claus has left all the things they asked for, in exchange for the drink and piece of cake they left out for him the night before. Carols (both traditional and contemporary, reflecting Christmas in the Pacific) are sung in the churches and, by candlelight, outdoors.

In New Zealand Christmas comes near the beginning of the long summer school vacation. As a result, many New Zealanders prefer to spend their Christmas on vacation, perhaps at the beach. More and more people, even if they stay at home, are abandoning the traditional roast meal and rich plum pudding and are opting for barbecues in the summer sun.

The 10-day Goldfields Heritage Celebrations, held every November in Otago, is an exciting affair. A horse-drawn gold coach travels the route of the old gold diggers, with each town visited holding their own celebrations.

Opposite: **Stilt walkers at the International Festival of the Arts.**

EASTER AND OTHER HOLIDAYS

Good Friday and Easter Monday are public holidays in New Zealand. Many Christians give up a favorite food during the 40-day period of Lent, which leads up to Easter, as it is a time when they remember the death of Jesus.

Special foods that are typical of Easter include hot currant buns topped with white icing in the shape of a cross, which are symbolic of Jesus' death, and chocolate eggs, symbolic of new life and Jesus' resurrection. Easter is also a time for special events, such as fairs, craft shows, car rallies, and club activities.

LABOR DAY was introduced in 1899 to commemorate the eight-hour working day. It falls on the fourth Monday each October.

SAMUEL DUNCAN PARNELL'S EIGHT-HOUR DAY

Parnell was an English settler determined to promote working conditions in New Zealand that were far better than those in his homeland. Soon after his arrival in New Zealand, he was asked to build a store for a shipping agent. He agreed, on condition he only worked eight hours every day, arguing that there are "twenty-four hours per day given us; eight of these should be for work, eight for sleep, and the remaining eight for recreation." Because tradesmen were scarce in the new settlement, the shipping agent agreed to Parnell's terms.

And so, Parnell wrote later, "the first strike for eight hours a day the world has ever seen was settled on the spot." Other employers tried to impose the traditional long hours, but Parnell met incoming ships, talked to the workmen, and enlisted their support—they agreed anyone offending the eight-hour rule was to be dunked in the harbor! Eventually the eight-hour working day became established.

QUEEN'S BIRTHDAY A public holiday is celebrated on the first Monday in June to mark Queen Elizabeth II's birthday, which is actually in April. Usually the only "celebration" involves the firing of 21 cannon balls as a salute to the queen.

NEW YEAR'S DAY is really celebrated in party style on New Year's Eve—leaving many people unable to celebrate the following day!

Each province also has its own anniversary day to mark its beginnings. From time to time, important events are re-enacted in period costume, such as the landing of the early settlers on the beaches of the capital city.

INTERNATIONAL FESTIVAL OF THE ARTS

Every two years an Arts Festival is staged in Wellington, which attracts high-caliber international artists and visitors from around the globe. For over three weeks, people can immerse themselves in every kind of artistic activity, from large-scale opera to mime and street artists. In 1994 there were over 400 performances involving 2,000 artists.

CREAMS
CHOCOLATE
STRAWBERRY
HOKEY POKEY
DEVON CREAM
$1.90 $2.40
one scoop   two scoops

FOOD

THE ARRIVAL OF IMMIGRANTS FROM EUROPE and the Middle East, and in particular from Asia and other parts of the Pacific, has altered the way New Zealanders think about their food. New and creative ways of food preparation and presentation have evolved from a blend of ethnic influences to produce what is now described as a Pacific Rim cuisine. Nonetheless, some traditional foods of the Maori have retained special meaning. For example, only the women of a certain tribe can eat the meat of the *kereru* ("ke-re-ROO"), or wood pigeon.

New Zealand is blessed with an abundance of meat, seafood, fruit, and vegetables. Its people take a real interest in food and wine, and throughout the year festivals are held to promote and enjoy the food produced in different regions. For example, the second Saturday in February is the time for the Wine and Food Festival in Marlborough (the northern region of the South Island).

Opposite: **Ice cream, anyone?**

Left: **Asian cornershops are an increasingly common sight, especially in the larger cities.**

113

Above: **A young New Zealander enjoys a quick meal.**

Opposite: **Greenshell mussels for sale.**

Marlborough is not only New Zealand's premier wine-growing district. It is also known as the gourmet's paradise because of the very diverse range of food produced there. In Marlborough the sounds yield tasty salmon, greenshell mussels, snapper, tarakihi, and blue cod, the coast delivers up succulent crayfish, while the clear lakes and rivers contain excellent rainbow and brown trout. Nearby the farms produce venison and lamb, and crops of olives, hazelnuts, and wasabi grow alongside cherries, apples, berries, and garlic.

People can enjoy the local delicacies in restaurants, or they may prefer to have a picnic, which might include a slab of snapper (marinated and smoked), a chunk of fresh herb bread, some olives, sun-ripened tomatoes, and zesty pickles and wine. Picnics are a favorite way of enjoying food outdoors during the summer months.

GREENSHELL MUSSELS

The greenshell mussel is unique to New Zealand, the shellfish deriving its name from the color of its shell. Most of the commercially exported mussels are farmed. A mussel farm consists of a series of buoys held together by long lines attached to each side of the buoy. The line is anchored to the sea floor at each end. From the long lines a series of weighed ropes hang down, but do not reach the bottom.

Young mussels attach themselves to the rope, aided initially at seeding out by being encased in a stocking mesh, which disintegrates a few weeks after being immersed in the sea. The mussels are then left to grow. After 14 to 18 months, when the mussels have reached the desired size, the rope is lifted and the mussels are harvested.

MUSSELS, WINE, AND CREAM

2 ¹/₂ cups (600 ml) dry New Zealand white wine
24 New Zealand greenshell mussels
2 leeks
4-inch (10 cm) piece of cucumber, seeded

1 ounce (25 g) butter
1¹/₂-inch (4 cm) piece of ginger, coarsely grated
⁵/₈ cup (150 ml) pint double cream
a pinch of saffron

Put white wine, together with any juices from the mussels, into a pan and boil until reduced by half. Cut leeks and cucumber into very fine 2-inch long (5 cm) julienne strips. Melt butter in a pan and gently fry leeks for 5 minutes. Add ginger and cucumber and fry for 3 minutes. Add reduced wine, cream, and saffron, bring to a boil, and add the mussels. Cover and simmer gently for about 5 minutes or until mussels are piping hot. Serves 4 as an appetizer, or 2–3 as a light main course.

Popular barbecue fare includes beef, lamb, or fish steaks, chicken kebabs, and sausages, accompanied by a variety of sauces, salads, and beer, fruit juice, or wine.

BARBECUES

The barbecue is very much part of the New Zealand lifestyle. New Zealanders spend a lot of leisure time socializing, visiting friends and relatives, and sharing food together. The outdoor "barbie" is a relaxed and informal way to enjoy food and company during the summer months and it is usually a time when women watch the men cook.

FISH AND CHIPS

Of all the fast foods and carry outs that are available to New Zealanders (including hamburgers and pizza), "fish-'n'-chips" are still the most popular. Introduced by the British, fish and chips consist of large portions of fish in batter and french fries sprinkled with salt and vinegar. Traditionally they were always wrapped in newspaper to take away, but today, more hygienic but less interesting wrapping is used.

MAORI FOOD TRADITIONS

The Maori people cooked their food in earth-ovens called *hangi* ("HAA-ngee"). A *hangi* is prepared by digging a pit, setting up a mountainous pile of wood in it, and then placing stones on top. The fire is then lit to heat the stones.

The stones are sprinkled with water to remove ash and create steam and the food is placed on leaves on top of the stones. After several hours of slow steaming, the food is tender and very tasty. Nowadays the word *hangi* also refers to the feast itself, which always follows the main ceremony at a *marae* gathering.

Two enterprising Maori women cook *kumara* to sell to tourists. Foods that cook well in a *hangi* include meat and vegetables that roast well, such as potatoes, *kumara*, yams, pumpkin, and parsnips.

LIFESTYLE FOOD

Most people in New Zealand cook with either electric or gas stoves. Kitchens are very well equipped and modern—often incorporating the latest European technology.

Family food is generally simply prepared and includes meat, fish, or poultry with potatoes, rice, or pasta, and several cooked vegetables or salads. The main course might be followed by a dessert, such as fresh fruit and ice-cream. More exotic and elaborate three- or four-course meals are served for dinner parties.

The culinary high point of the week used to be the traditional, English-style roast dinner prepared for lunch on Sundays. While many people still like to have roast beef, lamb, or chicken occasionally, the Sunday ritual has generally been replaced by lighter food.

Despite the fact that New Zealand supermarkets are full of a large variety of fresh fruit and vegetables and scores of different cuts of meat, more and more people are buying convenience foods to keep pace with their busy lifestyles.

Eating out is hugely popular, especially with younger, working people, and lunchtime is becoming a favorite time to indulge in fine food. An interesting lunch could include a crayfish and crab apple mousse wrapped in spinach, accompanied by fresh Pacific oysters topped with salmon caviar and a New Zealand Chardonnay wine. There are numerous restaurants, particularly in the cities, where diners can choose from a wide range of cuisines, including European (French, Spanish, Greek, Italian, Austrian), Asian (Chinese, Indian, Lebanese, Cambodian, Malay, Thai, Indonesian, Japanese), Mexican, and, of course, New Zealand seafood. Local and national competitions encourage chefs to be innovative and to reach high standards.

KIWIFRUIT

Kiwifruit is New Zealand's leading horticultural export. It was originally known as the Chinese gooseberry because of its origins in the Yangtze valley of China. Somehow the seeds of this subtropical plant arrived in New Zealand at the beginning of the century and they have thrived in the warmer areas of the North Island.

Over the years orchardists have found ways to improve the quality and quantity of their yield. The name was changed to kiwifruit when New Zealand started to export the fruit in the 1950s. New Zealanders like to use kiwifruit in fruit salads or as a decorative topping on a traditional dessert such as the pavlova (a sweet meringue cake).

A display of wines in a supermarket.

WINE

While New Zealand shares the same latitude as the major wine-producing areas in Europe—from the Rhine Valley in the north, through Alsace, Champagne, Burgundy, Loire, and Bordeaux in France, and into southern Spain—its climatic conditions are quite different. The long, narrow shape of New Zealand's two main islands means that no location is more than 80 miles (129 km) from the sea, giving it a maritime climate.

Most of the vineyards lie in coastal areas where they bask in an average of 2,200 sunshine hours each year and are cooled at night by sea breezes. This climatic pattern provides ideal growing conditions, producing premium-quality grapes.

Wine-making in New Zealand dates back to the earliest settlers. Pioneer missionary Samuel Marsden planted about 100 vines at his mission station in Kerikeri, Bay of Islands, in 1819. When James Busby, the British Resident and an expert viticulturist, arrived in 1833, he set about turning Marsden's grapes into wine.

Even the French navigator Dumont d'Urville was impressed with New Zealand wine, noting in his journal, "I was given a light white wine, very sparkling and delicious in taste, which I enjoyed very much."

The French Catholic missionary Bishop Pompallier also had an interest in wine and he established another vineyard. During the next few years, grape vines were taken to other parts of New Zealand by French missionary priests.

Hardworking immigrants from Yugoslavia and Lebanon laid the foundations of the modern New Zealand commercial wine industry early in the 20th century. But it was not until after World War II when New Zealand servicemen returned from Europe, having acquired a taste for European-style table wine, that wine-makers in New Zealand had a local market.

Since the 1960s, there has continued to be a rapid growth in wine production and consumption. The modern viticulturists have combined traditional vineyard practices with state-of-the-art techniques to enhance the flavor and produce wines with a distinctive New Zealand style. Today, New Zealand wine excites the world's judges and wine media commentators. In international competitions, New Zealand regularly wins high awards for its Sauvignon Blanc, Chardonnay, Cabernet/Merlot, and sparkling wines.

BEER

Beer drinking, especially among New Zealand males, was very popular a long time before the now fashionable wines appeared on the scene. Until 1967, licensing laws prohibited the sale of alcohol after 6 p.m. This led to frenzied drinking for 90 minutes after the factories and other work places closed for the day, causing what came to be known as "the six o'clock swill." Drinking hours were later extended, apparently in an effort to reduce drunkenness. Pubs can now stay open as long as they like.

The British explorer Captain James Cook pioneered brewing in New Zealand when he established a brewery at Dusty Sound. Today there are three primary breweries. New Zealand beer is similar to English- and Netherlands-style lagers with its own "Steinlager" being one of the most popular beers in New Zealand and abroad.

The West Coast region in the South Island is host to the Hokitika Wildfoods Festival—an extravaganza of gourmet "bush tucker" based on West Coast's natural food sources, including the huhu *("hoo-hoo") grub. The* huhu *beetle is New Zealand's largest native beetle—up to 2 inches (50 mm) long—and the* huhu *grub, which is found in dead wood, is a delicacy among the Maori.*

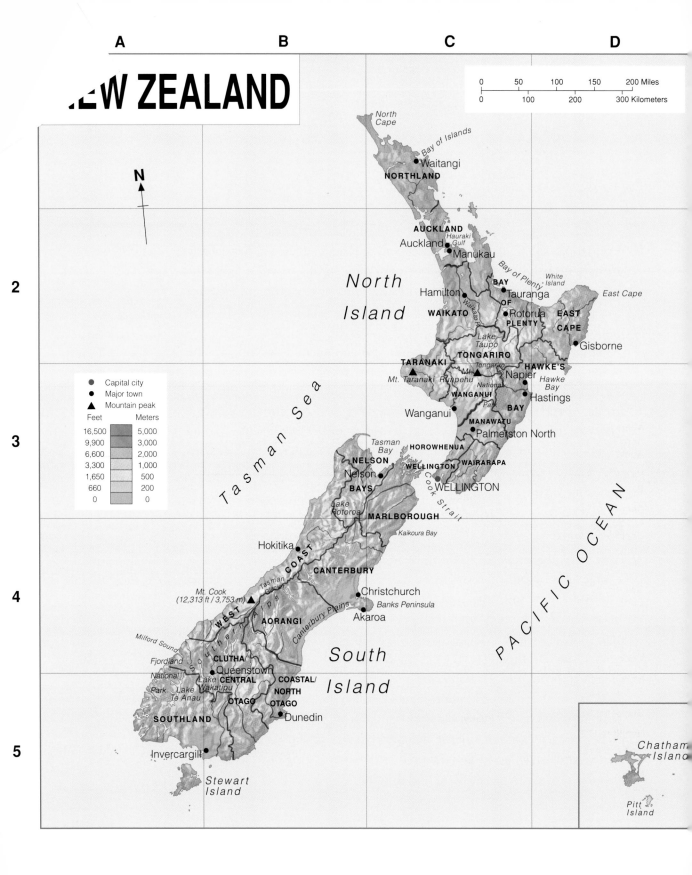

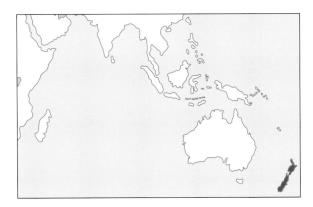

QUICK NOTES

OFFICIAL NAME
New Zealand

AREA
104,453 square miles
(270,534 square km)

POPULATION
3.6 million (1995)

CAPITAL
Wellington

OFFICIAL LANGUAGES
English, Maori

HIGHEST POINT
Mount Cook (12,313 ft / 3,753 m)

MAJOR LAKE
Lake Taupo

MAJOR RELIGION
Christianity

LONGEST RIVER
Waikato River

NATIONAL BIRD
The kiwi

NATIONAL FLOWER
Yellow flower of the kowhai tree

MAJOR CITIES
Auckland, Christchurch, Dunedin, Hamilton, Tauranga, Palmerston North, Napier

NATIONAL FLAG
Royal blue background with Union Jack in the first quarter and four five-pointed red stars of the Southern Cross on the fly. The stars have white borders.

CURRENCY
New Zealand dollar
1 dollar = 100 cents
US$1 = NZ$1.45

MAIN EXPORTS
Meat, dairy products, wool, forest products

MAJOR IMPORTS
Machinery and equipment, motor vehicles

POLITICAL LEADERS
Robert Muldoon, prime minister, 1975–84
David Lange, prime minister, 1984–89
Jim Bolger, prime minister from 1990

LEADERS IN THE ARTS
Dame Kiri Te Kanawa, Douglas Lilburn, Colin McCahon

ANNIVERSARIES
Waitangi Day (February 6)
ANZAC Day (April 25)
Queen's Birthday (first Monday in June)

GLOSSARY

Aorangi ("ah-or-rung-ee")
"Cloud piercer," Maori name for Mount Cook.

Aotearoa ("ah-or-te-ah-roar")
"Land of the long white cloud," Maori name for New Zealand.

haka ("huh-kuh")
Energetic, aggressive action song traditionally performed by men. Commonly performed today by the national rugby team, the All-Blacks, before a match.

hangi ("HAA-ngee")
Earth oven used by the Maori to cook food. Nowadays it also refers to the feast itself.

hapu ("huh-POO")
Sub-tribe.

hui ("hoo-ee")
Maori social and political gathering to which Europeans could be invited.

iwi ("ee-wee")
Tribe.

karanga ("kah-rah-ngah")
Call to visitors (always made by a woman) to enter the meeting house. The *karanga* is returned by a female leader on behalf of the visitors.

kumara ("KOO-mah-rah")
Sweet potato.

mana ("mah-nah")
Prestige, status, or honor.

marae ("mah-rye")
Social place where religious and secular activities take place. Rural Maori concept that has also been established in the cities.

moko ("mor-kor")
Tattoo—each person's tattoo was traditionally a form of identification.

pa ("PAA")
Earthwork fort commonly built by pre-European Maoris.

Pakeha ("PAA-ke-haa")
Maori term for the European settlers in New Zealand.

poi ("poy")
Small balls on the ends of strings used by female Maori performers.

tapu ("tuh-poo")
Maori word associated with Maori spiritual beliefs, meaning "sacred" or "holy."

tukutuku ("took-oo-took-oo")
The art of creating symbolic geometric designs using light, colored swamp reeds attached with flax cord to horizontal laths. Traditionally done by women.

whare ("fuh-re")
Traditional meeting house, the shape of which is believed to represent an ancestor's body.

whanau ("FAA-no-oo")
Extended family.

BIBLIOGRAPHY

Holden, Philip. *Station Country, Back-Country Life in New Zealand.* Auckland: Hodder & Stoughton Ltd, 1993.

Joyce, Ray; Saunders, Bill. *Discover New Zealand, The Glorious Islands.* Auckland: Landsdowne Press, 1982.

Lerner Publications. *New Zealand in Pictures (Visual Geography Series).* Minneapolis: 1990.

Sinclair, Keith. *The Oxford Illustrated History of New Zealand.* Auckland: Oxford University Press, 1996.

Whitney, Stewart; Keiser, Anne B. *Sir Edmund Hillary: To Everest and Beyond (Newsmaker).* Minneapolis: Lerner Publications, 1996.

INDEX

INDEX

INDEX